SHOW RING SUCCESS

Also by Kathleen Obenland

THE ARABIAN ENGLISH PLEASURE HORSE:
A GUIDE TO SELECTING, TRAINING AND SHOWING

SHOW
RING
SUCCESS

A RIDER'S GUIDE
TO WINNING STRATEGIES

Kathleen Obenland

HOWELL BOOK HOUSE

NEW YORK
MAXWELL MACMILLAN CANADA   TORONTO
MAXWELL MACMILLAN INTERNATIONAL   NEW YORK   OXFORD   SINGAPORE   SYDNEY

HOWELL BOOK HOUSE
MACMILLAN PUBLISHING COMPANY
866 THIRD AVENUE
NEW YORK, NY 10022

MAXWELL MACMILLAN CANADA, INC.
1200 EGLINTON AVENUE EAST
SUITE 200
DON MILLS, ONTARIO M3C 3N1

MACMILLAN PUBLISHING COMPANY IS PART OF THE MAXWELL COMMUNICATION
GROUP OF COMPANIES.

UNLESS OTHERWISE NOTED, ALL ILLUSTRATIONS ARE BY SHIRLEY DICKERSON

LIBRARY OF CONGRESS CATALOGING-IN-PUBLICATION DATA

OBENLAND, KATHLEEN.
SHOW RING SUCCESS : A RIDER'S GUIDE TO WINNING STRATEGIES /
KATHLEEN OBENLAND.
P.   CM.
INCLUDES INDEX.
ISBN 0-87605-965-5
1. SHOW RIDING.   2. HORSE-SHOWS.   I. TITLE.
SF295.2.O34 1993
798.2—DC20   93-15115 CIP

MACMILLAN BOOKS ARE AVAILABLE AT SPECIAL DISCOUNTS FOR BULK
PURCHASES FOR SALES PROMOTIONS, PREMIUMS, FUND-RAISING, OR
EDUCATIONAL USE. FOR DETAILS, CONTACT:

SPECIAL SALES DIRECTOR
MACMILLAN PUBLISHING COMPANY
866 THIRD AVENUE
NEW YORK, NY 10022

10 9 8 7 6 5 4 3 2 1

PRINTED IN THE UNITED STATES OF AMERICA

To AnnaMae Bartels

Contents

Acknowledgments

Thank you to the many people who shared their knowledge and talents in the creation of this book, including my family; equine artist Shirley Dickerson; judges David McKay, Hal Armstrong, Billy Harris and Ken Copenhaver; and especially Lynn "Ralph" Obenland, who meant so much to me and was always there for me.

Preface

I used to be one of those people who finished at the bottom of the class even at the smallest horse shows. My riding skills were terrible. My horses were poorly trained. When I finally got a riding instructor to give me some desperately needed help, she assessed my skills as "hopeless." I was riding for years before I ever won a trophy.

That's a pretty bad start, but nobody who gets on a horse for the first time rides well. Everyone starts at the same place—riding badly. Years later, some of those same people are winning national titles, while others are still placing last at backyard shows. The difference is what occurred in between. Years ago in those dusty practice arenas, something happened inside the riders who would one day win success. A desire kindled and began to burn with a steady, unswerving intensity. It heated them with the motivation and persistence to excel.

The other riders never felt it.

If you are reading this book, you are one of those who can feel the drive inside you. For me it was late in coming, but it did come. Over the years I went from losing classes at the county fair to winning national championships. That is a long way, but it is possible. Regardless of how you are doing now, you can significantly improve your riding and therefore your placings in the show ring. As your skills grow, you will be able to successfully compete at increasingly larger shows—including one day, perhaps, regional, district, national or world shows.

Success is self-made.

Winning riders create it for themselves—the key is knowing how they do it. Let this book serve as a map to help you find the paths they take. It contains the techniques, information and ring strategies that top riders learn over many years on the show circuit.

Show ring success is comprised of many different things. First, you have to want to ride well for the sake of riding well. If you just want to win a trophy you probably will not be able to keep up the effort long enough to actually get it.

You also have to have a love of horses that resonates through your entire being. If your love is genuine, it will deepen with time as the riding and horses become part of you. If it is not, you will grow tired of all the labor involved with owning and riding horses.

You must be patient with yourself and the horse, because progress is more often measured in inches than in yards and it is not always easy to see. Don't be discouraged. When you practice properly, you cannot help but improve. It is unavoidable. At some point you will look back and marvel at how far you have come. Stick with your efforts and believe in yourself. You are better than you think.

Don't dally around waiting for opportunities. Take the initiative. For example, if you need a riding instructor, go out and find one. Don't wait for someone to call asking if you want lessons. The call may never come.

Formulate a plan and set goals. This will keep your motivation alive and focus your efforts. Don't let yourself be sidetracked by excuses about why you can't do something. Of course you can do it. You just have to find a way. It is never too late or too early to improve your equine skills.

Successful riders don't let obstacles stop them. They steadily develop their craft. They practice frequently, seek out good teachers and educate themselves about horses and riding. They learn how to select the best horses, and they study the characteristics of other winning horses and riders.

People currently succeeding in the show ring were once where you are right now. You, too, can pull yourself up to the top.

SHOW
RING
SUCCESS

Do You Have
the Right Horse?

Selecting a horse is one of the most important decisions you will make affecting your show career. You are picking out the partner. You will invest in him all the time and emotion that comes with showing. He has to be worthy of that selection and able to meet your needs and expectations.

HORSES FOR BEGINNERS

Beginners should always buy well-trained, well-seasoned horses. When you are first starting out, the horse's training and ability to get along with you is more important than almost anything else. That includes even his appearance.

The best horse might have a drab color, too long a back or even a face that is a little bit ugly. Minor flaws like that are all right, as long as the horse is well trained and the two of you get along. Don't reject a good horse because he isn't the color you want, or isn't as pretty as you want. A horse's real beauty is in his abilities, not his looks. While beauty does play a role in performance classes, it is minor compared to those of ability and experience.

The only quality of equal importance to ability and experience is soundness. You don't want a horse that will continually go lame. Also keep in mind what classes you want to ride. His experience and skills should be in those classes. For example, if you want to ride English Pleasure, the horse you buy should be skilled in English.

Well-trained horses cost more than other horses, but the price is worth it. Young horses are usually less expensive initially, but not in the long run. If you are going to show the horse successfully, he has to be trained. By the time you pay for the young horse's training you probably will have spent as much as if you had bought the veteran. Professional training is essential. At your level of experience, you are not yet able to teach him all the things he needs to know. To be competitive he needs the trainer's expertise.

It is a commonly held belief in some circles that if you match an inexperienced horse with an inexperienced rider, the two can just learn together and train each other without professional guidance. That's one of the worst things you can do. It hampers the development of both the horse and the rider. It's like handing two students a calculus textbook and expecting them to learn together. They might figure it out in time, but the learning process would be much faster if you sent the student in with a teacher instead of another student. The same is true of riders. You'll learn more, faster, from a veteran horse than from one that knows less than you do. And the inexperienced horse will learn more, faster, from a trainer.

I tried the "learn together" approach myself. While the green horse and I were learning together, we were losing valuable time. My skill level, which was extremely dubious at the time, was progressing much more slowly than that of the riders who were learning on veteran horses. The horse I was riding ended up well broke, but not well trained.

As a matter of fact, there were two of these "learn together" horses. Both purchases were ridiculous. The first horse was wild. She'd been raised out in a pasture and rarely if ever touched by human hands. She was pretty, but probably the absolute worst purchase we could have made. We had been looking for a broke, tame horse that I could ride in my horse club. Instead we got carried away with appearances and bought a horse with a skill level even worse than mine.

We did the same thing with the horse that followed her. He was a much better horse, but he was untrained, and our reasons for choosing him over another were silly.

We had looked at a veteran of many shows, and passed him by because he was ugly. He was a ghastly, almost pink color and had a face like an ironing board. While he didn't have what it took to succeed at large shows, I wasn't ready for large shows. I needed a well-trained horse to help make me a well-trained rider. That's exactly what he was.

Someone else bought him and did quite well. I'm sure the rider learned a great deal from him, too. At the same time I was left struggling with Jay, a horse my family purchased because we liked the way he held up his tail when he moved. And so came another unnecessary delay in my learning the equine skills. Jay and I did learn a lot together, but each of us was held back by the other's lack of knowledge.

When horse shopping, scrutinize the horse's level of schooling every bit as much as the straightness of his legs. The horse should also have a quiet manner. Hot horses can be good show horses, but only for experienced riders. Most horses with high energy levels are extremely sensitive to the rider. A hot horse can't stand a rider who moves around on his back, has unstable hands or is intimidated by his energy. Don't buy a hot or untrained horse until you have the experience to handle one.

Also keep in mind that while you want a veteran, not every veteran qualifies as a good horse on which to learn. Some show horses can only be ridden by extremely experienced riders. But there are many horses that are patient and would be good mounts for you.

The veteran knows the cues you are supposed to give, how your weight distribution is supposed to feel and how you should hold the reins. He'll let you know if you are doing something wrong. Give him the wrong cue for the canter and he'll continue to plod along until you get close enough to the right cue for him to recognize it. Hold the reins too tight and he may refuse to take the gait you're asking for, or he may shake his head in protest. A well-schooled horse is one of the best riding instructors you will ever have. In the show ring, he can also help you achieve some success almost immediately. And that will help motivate you to continue riding and improving.

Experienced horses can be found if you have patience and make a concerted effort. Call the farms that show the breed you like, and say you want an experienced, quiet horse that can be ridden by someone at your stage of riding. Many veteran horses are also advertised for sale in breed magazines.

The horse does not have to be old to be a veteran. He can be fairly young, even six or seven, as long as he is patient and has had a lot of successful ring experience. When you think you have found him, make arrangements to ride him. Take someone with you who is experienced with horses—preferably the trainer or riding instructor who will be working with you and the horse. Have him or her ride the horse, too. If you don't know any trainers or instructors, call an experienced horse person you admire. Chances are he or she will help you.

HORSES FOR INTERMEDIATES

The experienced horse will be the best mount for you as well. This is particularly true if you have been riding for years but are about to make your first foray into higher-level showing.

You will be able to handle more of a horse than a beginning rider, but you can still benefit greatly from the things the experienced horse can teach you. He likely will offer you a greater chance for success than a young horse. If you choose to buy a green or unbroke horse, make sure you have help from a professional in training the horse.

When shopping, look for a horse that you can ride easily, has an appealing appearance, is athletic and has the conformation and ability for the classes you will use him in. This will be discussed in more detail in the following section.

The horse's show record should reflect a lot of success at the level you want to ride. Past success is an excellent way to gauge how well you might do with this horse in the future. You want a horse that can help you succeed at the larger shows, even perhaps at a regional or district level. With a lot of work and the right horse, an intermediate level rider can even qualify for national or world competition.

There are many good horses available. Call around, talk to horse people, watch the breed magazines and take your time to find the right horse. It will also be worth your while to go to the better shows in your area. If you see a horse that would suit you, talk to the owners. They may be willing to sell. Even if you don't find a horse, attending the shows is good for your education.

Before you buy, it is a good idea to have another experienced horse person look at the horse, too.

No matter how nice the horse is, don't buy him if you can't ride him. Someone else may have ridden him well and easily, but your ability to ride him is what counts. You are the one about to enter into a long-term partnership with this horse. You and the horse will be miserable if you can't get along.

If you want a horse you can ride, *buy* a horse you can ride.

HORSES FOR EXPERIENCED RIDERS

The horse you want is an exceptional individual that can take you to the top of the class in regional, district, national or world competition. When you are capable of riding at a high level, you need a horse capable of winning at that level.

That doesn't mean you throw away the things you considered important when you were less experienced. You just build on them.

The horse must be sound and built for the task you have in mind. Even within the confines of a single breed there are many different builds of horse. Each build is for a specific purpose, such as Western Pleasure or English Pleasure. Purchase a horse that shows great ability in the classes you want to ride. Training can develop ability, but it cannot take its place. If you buy a horse that is not properly built for the classes you want to ride, you will never be happy with him. He will be physically unable to do what you want at a competitive level.

The horse should also have a good attitude. Look for a horse that goes about his work with gusto and a pleasant, interested expression. If his ears are pinned most of the time or he has an angry expression on his face, he is being forced by his rider. Even if the horse is otherwise very nice, don't buy him if he exhibits a bad attitude. He will be hard to get along with, and his attitude will hurt your placings in the ring.

A high-level show horse must also have great appeal. While beauty is a factor, even more important than that is presence. A horse can be beautiful and still bland. But a horse with a commanding presence will draw the judges' eyes to him again and again, even if he is not classically beautiful. The horse knows how special he is, and that radiates throughout his entire being in every expression, every motion. You cannot help but look. It is the same quality that exists in great movie stars. That look of a star is an integral part of the very best show horses.

When you see it, you will recognize it. It is the quality that, if you have looked at horses all day, causes one specific horse to stick in your mind. Take your time looking and don't buy until you find that special individual.

Try out any horse you are considering buying. It's not wise to buy a horse straight from a magazine ad or video. You may be very experienced, but not every person gets along with every horse. When you find the horse you want, have a veterinarian examine him thoroughly. Do not buy him unless he checks out as healthy and sound.

The price you pay will depend on the breed of horse, level of training, type of training, the horse's show record and the mood of the market.

At your level of experience, the horse's age will probably be relevant only in the length of time you will have to wait before you can show him at a high level. If you buy a mature, finished horse, you can take him in the ring immediately. If you buy a youngster, you may have to wait a while before his training and maturity allow him to be competitive. Immature horses have a tough time competing against mature ones.

Working with a young horse can be a wonderful experience for you. If the youngster you find is exceptional, he will be worth the wait and all the time you put into him. You can do much of the breaking and training yourself. I would still recommend, however, that a professional trainer do the finishing. If you are going to show him at a reasonably competitive level, he will need the professional finish. Professional trainers spend all day, every day, working horses. As experienced as you are, they are even more experienced in knowing how to bring out the very best in a horse.

. . . .
SHOW HORSE PERSONALITIES

Another aspect often overlooked in selecting a horse is his mental characteristics. Some horses are better mentally equipped than others for the show ring. Some mental characteristics even make a horse prone to fail at showing, burn out early, or never reach full potential.

Good show horses tend to be bold and self-assured and have an internal drive to please their riders. They are charismatic, bright and curious and adapt quickly to new circumstances. They are willing students and take well to training.

You can see these characteristics expressed in many ways. Horses that have them tend to have a perceivable cockiness. You can tell by the way they conduct themselves that they think highly of themselves. The cockiness usually is accompanied by boldness. Bold horses are aggressive and are undaunted by having to work in crowds of horses. They will move through dense groups with ease. Extremely bold horses behave as if clad in iron. For example, if you were riding in the practice arena and it looked like you might collide with an oncoming horse, the extremely bold horse would not waver. If you wanted him to veer off, you would have to tell him so. He would be more likely to continue forward, assuming the other horse should give ground to him.

Horses destined to be good in the ring aren't often easily upset. While training naturally causes anxiety at times, the horse usually does not become more overwrought than the situation merits. He is also likely to recover quickly from being anxious, tense or frightened. Many good show horses are, by horse standards, pretty brave. While the show lifestyle promotes this, you can see the trait in some young horses, too.

You can try a bravery test with your horses at home. Take a household throw rug or sheet of black plastic out to your pasture, drape it over the fence, then sit and watch what happens. The test works best with a group of horses of approximately the same age. The horses will notice the rug or plastic with a sudden shock and scatter away. Then they'll band closely together at a safe distance and stare at it. Soon you will find out which is the brave one. You might think it would be the most dominant horse, but that isn't always the case. One horse will break away from the group and go to check out the horrible thing on the fence. The others will follow at a safe distance to see what happens to him. After he establishes that it is not dangerous, the others will go up one by one and sniff it. While all of the horses may turn out to be good show horses, you now know which one at this point in time shows the most bravery, curiosity and ability to adapt to the unusual.

Another important characteristic in show horses is hard to see until after you start working the horse. Riders call it "heart." It means that the horse will not quit on you. He won't decide he's done enough and refuse to do more. A horse with heart keeps going. He'll try as hard as he can for as long as he possibly can. A horse with this attitude is capable of brilliant performances because he is willing to give his all. A quitter can rarely match such an effort because he's only willing to give so much.

Undesirable traits to look out for in a horse are timidity, frequent anxiety, lack of intelligence, dullness and bad temperament.

Timidity is the least serious of these traits. A timid horse has a more difficult time becoming a show horse because the dynamics of the show ring require some boldness. A horse that is intimidated by other horses is likely to perform badly when the show ring is crowded. His timidity may also make him afraid of new places. But he can overcome it if he has other positive traits. If he is willing to give his best effort, he can still succeed. These horses take a special kind of rider, a calm, quiet rider who can gain the horse's trust and help him through the difficult times.

Nervous horses prone to frequent anxiety, however, probably won't survive long as show horses. They cannot endure the strain of training or showing. These are the kind of horses that may start sweating from nerves before the workout even begins, and may become more agitated than situations seem to warrant. Under pressure they tend to fall apart, becoming so anxious they cannot perform even the simplest task correctly until they calm down. They may develop stall vices as well, such as constant circling. Sometimes nervous horses do hold together long enough to make it in the ring, but they rarely last.

Please note, however, that an anxious horse is not the same thing as a hot horse. Hot horses are quite sensitive, quick to react and energetic. The heat gives them a flamboyance beneficial in some classes. While it is possible for a horse to be so mindlessly hot he is hard to train, that is not the case for most hot horses. They just need riders who understand how to manage and channel their energy.

Unintelligent horses, on the other hand, present a lot of training problems. Some horses learn a lot more quickly than others, while there are some that have trouble learning even the most basic of tasks. You may be able to get one of these horses into the ring, but it will cost you a great deal in training fees and time.

The dull horse has a different problem. By dull, I mean a horse lacking in charisma, interest, brightness and drive to succeed. He's trainable, but it's unlikely he'll do anything particularly well. He lacks the thing inside him that drives the good horses to put all they have into a performance. It's just not there, and you can't train it in. The best way of detecting a dull horse is just to trust your gut feelings. He will be the one that will seem somehow bland, even if his color is nice. His facial expressions will tend to be dull or vacant. Looking at him, you won't be left with much of an impression at all.

The final trait to avoid is a bad disposition. Such horses are cranky, obnoxious and sometimes mean. They are hard to work and may resist training, and they are a trial to own. Some do become successful show horses, but since you could as easily have a pleasant, well-mannered show horse, what is the point of buying an obnoxious one?

STEPPING UP

As your riding improves, so should your horses. You usually will not hit the highest peaks of competition with the same horse on which you learned to ride. It is common to own a number of horses, riding each until your skill level allows you to move on to more competitive horses.

It can be hard to part with the horse you have outgrown, but if you do not he will hold you back. He can no longer keep up with your skill level. Rather than trying to continue with him, it is better to retire him to pleasant pasture life or let him carry a new rider into the ring. He can help another person become a better rider the same way he helped you.

The new horse you buy should not just be a replacement. He should be a significant advancement. His skills and abilities should improve your placings and carry you to larger shows. For example, let's say you have been doing well at the small shows and are ready for another horse. If you buy a horse that has also been doing well at small shows, you will not have improved your situation much. You will have stayed in the same place you were. But if you bought a horse that was competitive at larger shows, you would be stepping up toward higher levels of showing.

The horse really can help determine your levels of showing. When you buy a horse that has been successful at large shows, chances are you will show there. The next steps up are regional or district shows, then national or world competition. If you want to someday compete in national or world competition, the horse you select can help you move closer to that goal. You will have to work just as hard to get there, but it may not take as long or involve as many steps.

The horse you buy can also create alliances between you and the barns, trainers and other people who can help you reach your goals. A person who buys a horse from a training facility commonly has the option of becoming a new client. This can be a good deal for you. You can take lessons and the horse can get periodic training tuneups before important shows.

If, instead, you buy the horse from a respected individual, you may get just as many benefits. Many people are willing to assist someone who has purchased one of their horses. The former owners can be great resources to you. They can help you find a riding instructor and get into a training facility that will keep the horse tuned.

In some cases, your willingness to make use of a trainer or riding instructor will determine whether or not you will be sold the horse. Some owners will only sell their seasoned show horses to people who will show, use a trainer and take riding lessons. This is not snobbishness. The owners care for their horses and want the best for them. They know if you are receiving help with the horse, your relationship with him will be more successful. Then everyone, including the horse, will profit.

BONDING WITH A NEW HORSE

The relationship between a horse and rider is very special. Knowing your horse well increases your confidence in the ring, and that increases his. You know exactly how he feels when he is going well, and how much rein and leg to use to help him along. You've seen him at his worst, his best and everything else in between. He knows you just as intimately. He knows every shift of your weight, every cue and all the emotions that pass through you. He can feel when you are nervous, jubilant or angry.

The chemistry between the horse and rider can even become tangible, like the chemistry between dance partners. That doesn't happen with every horse. Some you will not get along with at all, and some you will only know in a vaguely pleasant way. But then there are the ones that embrace your soul. With those horses you have the chance for a special experience. Your bond with the horse will show in the ring. And your pleasure at being with him will make practice and showing more enjoyable. The victories will seem better, and the defeats not as bad.

Just like friendship, the bond may be almost instantaneous, or develop over time. Your first encounters with the horse may even be unpleasant. My first ride on the National Show Horse, Dutch Dolly, ended with me on the ground picking gravel out of my hands. The next few encounters weren't much better, although I did manage to stay on. But in the months that

The bond you develop with your horse is important to your riding success and enjoyment of showing. Spend as much time as possible with your horse.

followed, I developed a great affection for her and came to admire her energy and heart. On her I felt invincible in the ring, and it showed.

The best way to learn about your horse and bond with him is to spend lots of time with him. Ride him in and out of the ring. Play with him, talk to him. Do a lot of grooming, especially brushing (see illustration, page 11). Scratch him in all those wonderful places that make his lips tremble with pleasure, such as at his withers and under his mane. Feed him snacks.

He does not feel emotions in the same way that you do, but both humans and horses are social animals. The two of you can develop the bond of companionship, confidence in one another, trust and closeness.

. . . .
IMPROVING YOUR PRESENT HORSE

The horse you are riding now may have the ability to take you at least part of the way to your goal.

The first horse I won a national championship with was purchased green broke just as something for me to ride until we could find a better horse. But under training, his true potential rose to the surface. The horse, Firetok, gave me my first national championship at age five, when he was still a baby, and his prize money winnings that year nearly surpassed my annual salary. He now has multiple national wins in the United States and Canada.

These kinds of things don't happen every day, but they do happen. There are horses out there that are waiting to bloom to their full potential, and yours may be one of them. All you have to do is explore his talents.

Horses have talents just like people do. While you may be riding the horse in many different classes, he probably is better at some than others. In high competition, horses usually only go in a few classes or just one class, rather than a whole range. It's a practice that allows training to be concentrated on what the horse does best. His body develops the specific muscle tone and functions related to the class, and his mind absorbs the specific lessons. The horse is then able to do his best possible in that class.

With some classes, a mature horse's talent will be fairly obvious. (With youngsters it may be more difficult to spot.) It may not be clear how well the horse will do in the class, but someone who is knowledgeable about the class could tell you if the horse has an aptitude for it or not. Firetok, for example, had a high trot. That showed an aptitude for the saddleseat type of English Pleasure, where high knee and hock action is sought.

A horse with an aptitude for reining or cutting classes would be athletic and quick on his feet. A horse with an aptitude for western might have a smooth, fluid grace about his gaits. A horse with an aptitude for hunt might have a long, sweeping trot with little flex to the knee.

Your horse may already have told you what he does best. It may or may not be the same class that is your best. If you want him to be the best he can, you will have to accommodate his talents instead of forcing him through classes he does poorly. If you want to bring out the best in your mount, listen to him. What do his attitude and physical abilities say about his potential? Whether or not you can determine this, the next step is the same. Seek an outside opinion.

There are a number of ways to do this. Probably the most used, most reliable and most expensive way is to send the horse to a respected trainer for a sixty-day evaluation. At the end of that time, the trainer should have a good idea if the horse is going to succeed or not. Selecting a trainer will be discussed in a later chapter.

If you're uncertain of the horse's abilities and you're apprehensive about paying to find out what they are, that's all right. It is possible to get an estimation of the horse's talent without spending much money. Then, if it seems like he might be talented after all, you can send him in for a more extensive evaluation with the trainer.

Your first step is to select a knowledgeable equestrian to look at the horse. He or she after seeing the horse may know where the horse's best skills lie, or may be able to tell you who else should look at him.

Show the horse under saddle to your guest. (If the horse isn't broke, turn him loose.) Then ask your guest if the horse is well suited for the class you are riding him in. If the answer is yes, ask at what level he could successfully compete. If the answer is no, ask why, and what class the horse might be better suited for. Then ask at what level the horse could compete in that class.

Go through this process with a number of in-the-know people. One person's opinion isn't enough. It is good to get a selection, then listen to what the majority is saying. It will give you good information and help you better understand the horse's strengths and weaknesses.

You can often get these assessments done without spending much. At a show, round up some knowledgeable people and ride the horse for them. You don't even have to be competing at the show to do this. Just take the horse and show him to the people you want to see him.

Another method is to call knowledgeable people and ask if they would be willing to look at the horse. Sometimes you will have to take the horse to them, but it can be worth the drive.

A third way is to videotape the horse working, then send the tape to people, asking their opinion of him. This will cost you postage and the price of the tapes, but it is the best way to gather opinions from distant people.

Keep in mind when using any of these methods that how well the horse performs depends not only on talent, but also physical condition, age and training. Young horses can be hard to evaluate. So can horses that are out of shape and mired in obesity.

The opinions you gather will help affirm or deny your impression of the horse's abilities. Listen to what the people tell you, even if it is something you don't want to hear. They are doing you a favor by being candid. They may be wrong, but you should consider the fact that they may not be. Your vision of the horse may be clouded by your love for him. You may be seeing what you want to see instead of what is there. But you will not be doing him a favor by trying to force him to be a high-caliber show horse when he simply can't. Accept his limitations and do not try to make him something he is not. It will make both of you unhappy.

On the other hand, you may receive high praise for the horse. The next step, then, is to decide what you are going to do about it. Chances are for the horse to reach full potential in the show ring he will need a trainer. If you want that shot at success, you must be willing to part with him for periods of time so he can be with the trainer. There will also be training bills to pay.

. . . .

THE PLASTIC HORSE

As you climb higher in competition, you will begin seeing the plastic horses.

A plastic horse is one that never leaves the trainer's barn. You never take him home. You never get the chance to groom him, feed him or clean his stall. You never take him out on a trail ride or even to a show the trainer does not attend. You never do anything with him except for an occasional practice session under the trainer's supervision.

Your primary contact with him is in the show ring. When it's over you dismount and a groom leads the horse away. Your horse becomes like a plastic statue that you dust off once in a while to play with. You can own him for years without ever knowing him well.

Although the plastic horse constantly has a fine professional finish, there are a lot of drawbacks. It can leave you as the rider feeling as though something is lacking. It can create a feeling of distance between you and the horses, lessen your enjoyment of showing and make your ring work some-what tentative. It's like trying to have a successful long-distance romance.

Plastic horses are created by you and your trainer. If you buy a horse you cannot ride or can only ride long enough to get through a class, you have just created a plastic horse. There are some horses that need such a high level of rider skill that they get along only with trainers. Those horses spend their lives with trainers.

If you want to be an active part of the horse's life, there are inherent problems with having this kind of horse. Even a wonderfully talented horse can be a source of constant frustration if he is more than you can handle. You will sweat through each class, wondering what bad thing he is going to do next to cost you the win. You may also never be truly tuned in to him because you will only ride him at shows and at occasional practices under the trainer's supervision. With a horse that is particularly difficult, the trainer may encourage you to ride him as little as possible because he gets worse the longer you are on him.

I had an English mare like that. She found me such an annoyance that she and I kept our contacts short. The majority of time I was on her was when we were in the show ring. She was greatly talented and won a lot for me, but she and I never had much fun together. She was so unpredictable that I rode every class with my teeth on edge.

If you are going to buy a horse like this, at least know what you are getting into. The horse's talent may make the sacrifice worth while, but give it considerable thought.

Most horses don't have to be plastic. Even horses that need to be kept extremely sharp for competition usually don't have to be with the trainer all the time. Some trainers encourage their owners to leave the horse with them all year, but it usually isn't necessary.

Unless there is an overriding reason to leave the horse with the trainer, take him home for the off season. Take good care of him during those months and get to know him. It will be good for both of you and will keep him from becoming a plastic horse.

WHAT YOU CAN DO RIGHT AWAY TO IMPROVE

- Make a list of your horse's best abilities to help you determine what classes he excels in.
- Arrange to have him evaluated by at least three knowledgeable people to see if he may have potential to show at higher levels.

WHAT YOU CAN DO IN THE FUTURE

- Study conformation and how the horse should be built for specific kinds of work. Books on conformation are available at libraries, bookstores and tack shops. Experienced horse people are also a wealth of information about form-to-function and conformation.
- Attend one or more horse shows to observe the qualities of successful horses.
- When you start shopping, take your time and try a lot of horses before you buy one. Consider all the qualities you want in a new horse, taking into account your skill level and needs.
- Have a knowledgeable horse person look at your choice before you buy.

Shopping for a Riding Instructor or Trainer

One of the greatest things you can do to improve your riding is to accept help from other people. Even professional trainers and instructors seek advice and assistance from other professionals.

A riding instructor is essential. While there are many other elements in your equine education—including reading, watching instructional videos, attending shows and seeing good riders and horses perform—nothing can take the place of having someone observe and comment on your riding.

At some point you may find yourself in need of a trainer as well. The reality of the show ring today is that there are few horses that can reach high levels of competition without a trainer. Competition in many breeds has become so stiff that using a trainer is commonplace. Even at small, unrated shows, many of the horses have at some point been worked by professionals.

A riding instructor works mainly with you. A trainer works mainly with the horse. Your trainer and instructor (assuming you want both services) may be different people or the same person. Some professionals can handle either task with equal skill. Others deal only with one. For sake of discussion, we'll assume the instructor and trainer are separate people.

. . . .
AN INSTRUCTOR'S ROLE

If you are in a riding group you may be receiving instruction already. Chances are you would benefit from more. It is like hiring a tutor to help you in a class at which you particularly want to excel.

A riding instructor can do a myriad of things for you. He or she teaches much more than the mechanics of riding a horse. A good instructor can also teach you how to get the most out of a horse, show ring etiquette, handling difficult situations in the ring and grooming. I've had instructors who have covered everything from applying makeup to handling overcrowding in a ring. There are many aspects to looking good and performing well in the show ring. Every aspect has merit and is worth learning. Even seemingly minor points can make a big difference when competition is close.

Shopping for a good instructor is a lot like shopping for a good horse. You need to know what you want in an instructor before you begin. Your decision will be based on many things, including your goals as a rider. Ask yourself what level you want to be riding at within the next year. If you are riding at small local shows, you won't be ready for the regional championships in the next year, but you will be able to do better at your current level or perhaps advance to a little larger show. Also consider the level you want to be riding at in five years. In other words, what are the equine goals you want the instructor to help you meet?

Your selection will also be guided by the type of riding you do. This might be Hunt Seat Equitation, Western Equitation, Western Pleasure, Saddleseat Equitation, saddleseat-style English Pleasure, sidesaddle, or any number of classes. Instructors tend to be better in some classes than others. You also want one that is working with students riding at the level you are, or slightly above that level.

Many students make better progress if they concentrate their lessons on a specific class or two, rather than trying to do all of them. This is particularly true of those who have not been riding long. There is nothing wrong with trying to do it all. But few people excel at everything they do. Most excel where they apply the most effort. Choose one or two classes where you will put your greatest efforts. That may not sound like many, but it allows you to bring all your efforts to bear on one area so you can be great in one, rather than okay in a lot.

That doesn't mean you have to stop riding in the other classes. Every form of riding is good for you. It just means the bulk of your work goes to one or two classes. As you get better in those classes, you will find you are improving in the others as well because your riding skills are getting better on the whole. You probably will not be as good in the other classes as you are in your specialties, but you will do better in all of them. The basic principles behind riding well and getting a good performance out of the horse do not vary much from class to class.

To decide what to specialize in, ask yourself what classes you particularly enjoy and what classes your horse does particularly well in.

CHOOSING AN INSTRUCTOR

Choose an instructor with a great deal of experience in the classes in which you want to specialize. (Some riders even have several instructors—one for each area of specialization.) Ask around, take your time and choose carefully. Start your quest by studying your competitors. Who in your classes, or the classes you wish to be in, does well? Who do you admire? Who always looks sharp and skilled on his or her horse? Ask those people who is instructing them. Don't be afraid to approach them with the question. They will not be offended. It is fairly common for one instructor to have many students in a class. Your question will not be perceived as a threat. And don't let your competitors' success intimidate you into being afraid to talk to them. Most horse people will gladly talk to anyone about anything relating to horses.

Make note of the instructors' names you are given and what you are told about them. Then talk to the instructors either on the phone or at an equine event. While your choice of instructors will be partially influenced by how far away he or she is from you, don't let that be the overriding concern. A good instructor who is far away will do you more good than a mediocre one who is close. You will get more out of infrequent lessons from a good instructor than frequent lessons from a mediocre instructor.

Also, don't immediately think that a big-name instructor wouldn't consider accepting you as a student. You could be that person's next rising star. With hard work, persistence and a good horse, you can accomplish almost anything. Give yourself and the instructor a chance. You lose nothing by making that phone call to inquire. If you are turned down, just call another instructor.

Questions to ask when you talk to the instructor include:

- *What are the instructor's qualifications?* Ideally, the instructor will have a long history with the classes in which you are particularly interested. The instructor does not necessarily have to be presently riding in the classes— some instructors no longer ride. But it is important that he or she knows a great deal about them.
- *Who are some of his or her more successful students in the classes in which you are interested?* You may want to talk to a few of them as well.
- *How far have they gone in competition?*
- *What is the cost of the lessons, and what does the fee cover?* Some charge just an hourly rate to give the lesson, but all other services are free. Others charge additional fees for every service, including looking at a new horse with you and coaching you at a show. Matters of this type may be spelled out in a contract between you and the instructor, but not all instructors use contracts. If a contract is not used, make sure going into the relationship that you understand all the charges and what they are for. Ask for a list of fees.
- *Does the instructor have a lesson horse?* This is a horse, usually owned by the instructor, that you can take lessons on. This question is only pertinent if you will not have access to your own horse during lessons, as will be the case if your horse is in training at another, distant stable. While it is ideal to have a good portion of your lesson time on your own horse, it is not always possible.
- *Does the instructor offer flexible lesson hours?* If you work, go to school, have a family or other obligations, you will need an instructor who can offer you lessons at the times you need them, such as after work or on weekends.
- *Does the instructor have any conflicts of interest that would interfere with your show schedule?* Some instructors also are horse show judges. The American Horse Shows Association forbids people from showing under judges with

whom they have personal or financial relationships. If your instructor is a judge, you will not be able to attend shows where he or she is judging. It is not a reason to rule out hiring the person as an instructor. It is just a point you need to be aware of.

- *Will the instructor go to the shows with you if you request it?* You may want him or her there for large shows.
- *What kind of facility does the instructor have?* Ideal is an indoor arena with lights if you live in an area that gets a lot of rain and snow. Practice isn't just a summer sport. You need somewhere that you can practice all year round.

When selecting an instructor, it is also a good idea to watch him or her give a lesson. Observe the approach, suggestions and overall manner. Is this someone you can work with and accept criticism from? You are going to pay him or her to tell you about your riding flaws and strengths and how to improve. You need an instructor whose manner makes criticism just the first step to improvement.

You need someone you can listen to without feeling angry, torn down or persecuted. It is difficult at times to accept criticism or advice, but it is also necessary for improvement. Choosing the right instructor will make it easier. A good lesson is interesting and helpful. The lessons should leave you feeling that you are learning a lot. You should also feel that you can talk freely with your instructor about your riding. All of these qualities are part of lessons given by a skilled instructor. There are many good instructors. The right one can bring tremendous improvements in your riding and open up new horizons for you.

But make your choice with care. Not every riding instructor deserves the title; there are, unfortunately, some who simply are not that qualified. Unlike schoolteachers, riding instructors don't have to be certified or pass any test of qualifications. If you wanted, you could call yourself a riding instructor, advertise your services and begin giving lessons.

To improve your riding, you need an instructor who is genuinely qualified and highly skilled. It is also important to continually review how well you are progressing under the instructor and if he or she is meeting your needs. Sometimes problems arise.

You should consider changing instructors if the lessons make you feel inept or the instructor harshly berates your riding. You should also not tolerate an instructor who loses his or her temper and screams at you during lessons or after you have made a mistake in the ring. Anger is not a good teaching tool. A good instructor is patient and even tempered. For you to progress well in your lessons, you must develop confidence in yourself and the horse. It is difficult to do that with an instructor who is verbally abusive. You have the right as a student to be treated well. Good instructors should offer moral support, and tell you as much about what you are doing well as what you are doing badly. That information is essential to the learning process.

If you dread the lessons or they leave you upset or depressed, you need a different instructor. That is also true if you are intimidated by the instructor. You need someone you can talk to easily, and who you are not afraid of making errors in front of.

There are a number of other warning signs you should look out for that indicate an instructor isn't right for you. One is lack of knowledge—the instructor doesn't know things that you believe he or she should, or frequently tells you things that turn out to be incorrect. The instructor may also simply fail to answer your questions.

The instructor's other students leaving abruptly is another sign of trouble. Something probably is amiss. Talk to the other students to determine why they left.

Perhaps the most blatant sign that you are using the wrong instructor would be if he or she suggests something be done to the horse that you believe would be harmful or against show ring rules. Unfortunately, some people abuse and illegally drug horses. You do not want to be associated with anyone who would do that. Your horse could be next if he is in the instructor's care. And if the instructor is caught by show authorities, he or she could also be suspended from competition, and so could the entire barn of horses, including yours.

If you have any serious concerns about your instructor, find another. Having an instructor is important to your development as a rider.

BEING A GOOD STUDENT

To get the most out of the lessons, talk to the instructor and ask questions. Tell the instructor about any areas you particularly want to work on. If you don't understand something, such as how to use your legs to help the horse around a corner, stop and have the instructor explain it in more detail. Keep asking until you understand completely. Don't sit quietly and guess your way through the lessons. Become an active participant.

Combining your knowledge as a rider with the instructor's experience and observations is often the best way to solve problems with the horse's behavior or performance. The three of you—rider, horse and instructor—are a team. Problems are more easily solved if all of you are involved in the effort. While the instructor may be able to pinpoint the problem alone, he or she is missing important information—the rider's perception. The instructor can only go on what is seen, and that is not always enough to correctly determine what went wrong. Help your instructor by volunteering your own views of the problem. Don't wait to be asked. And if you think the instructor is wrong about his or her assessment of the problem, say so, and tell him or her why.

For example, let's say your horse often picks the canter up promptly and in the correct lead. But sometimes he fusses, trots sloppily into the canter and occasionally even gets the wrong lead. If you want do well at the shows, you must learn why sometimes he is so good, and other times so bad.

It's not correct to simply assume that you are doing something wrong or that the horse is. You must uncover the true cause. Discuss with the instructor in very specific terms what each of you noticed during the error. When the horse failed to go into the canter correctly, what exactly did he do? How did he feel to you? What were you doing with your hands, legs and weight? What did the instructor observe you doing? What did the instructor observe the horse doing? Is the horse making the error in the same place in the arena every time? What was the horse saying during the error? (In other words, were his ears up or back? Was he tensed or relaxed? Was he tired or energetic? Did he seem angry, bored or distracted? Did he seem indifferent or was he trying hard? Was his body compact or strung out long?)

By going through this process with the instructor, you can usually determine the real reason for the problem. It is then easier to fix. It could be that the horse is being lazy. In that case, when he fails to pick up the canter immediately, he should be stopped, kicked sharply in the ribs, then asked again. He must learn to always obey a cue instantly. But it also could stem from other reasons. Perhaps your cues are too inconsistent for him to recognize every time. You may need to concentrate more closely on your cuing. Or perhaps you are consistent at first, then lose consistency as you become tired. In that instance, you might want to shorten your lessons, and work at home on building your endurance. Perhaps the horse is getting distracted by things outside the arena. In that case, you would want to take a moment before cuing to make sure you have his attention. Perhaps he only fails to pick up the canter well going into a corner. It may take some experimenting to find out why. You might be leaning a little in anticipation of the corner or he might not be sufficiently balanced. Keep in mind, too, that as you near a corner, the horse is heading directly toward a fence in front of him. It may seem to him you are asking him to canter into a barrier.

There are many explanations for a horse's performance and behavior problems. Some causes are obvious, but others are not. If you discipline the horse without knowing why he is behaving badly, you run the risk of making the problem worse, confusing him or being more harsh than is necessary. Give both yourself and the horse the benefit of the doubt and work with the instructor to find the true cause of the problem so you can correct it properly.

The same approach should be used when refining your performance and that of the horse. Work together with the instructor to determine what works best. The principles of sound riding and training practices are fairly well established, but within them there is a lot of variation. Horses and people are individuals. Riding and training must take into account the differences brought into the ring by the skills, personalities and experiences of every horse and rider. Just as every horse feels and responds a little differently to each rider, every rider feels and responds differently to each horse.

Between lessons practice what you have learned. As problems crop up or questions arise during practice, you may want to jot down a few notes. You can talk to the instructor about these at your next lesson. Remember that the instructor is there to help you with any horse-related matter. You may want to seek his or her guidance about any number of topics, including what you should wear in the ring, what type of bit to use, or how long to warm up the horse before classes.

It takes a great deal of work and time to become a good rider. You must also overcome many frustrations. Even after you learn the lesson, it must seep down into your physical responses before you can apply it consistently and properly. It's like making coffee. Even after you add all the necessary ingredients to the coffee machine, you still have to wait a while before the water drips down through the grounds and becomes coffee. There will be times when as a rider you will know exactly what to do, but will be unable to get your body to perform the task properly. With further practice, however, your physical responses will catch up.

Much of riding is a series of almost automatic responses you teach your body. Your brain learns them first, then you do them over and over until your body will perform the tasks without you having to concentrate on every move. It's like learning to write. When you first began, you had to think about the shape of each letter and then draw it. Forming all of those lines and circles into letters and words took the utmost concentration. Now you scarcely think about it. Your hand writes the letters as soon as your mind conceives the words. Practice, education and time make all the difference in every endeavor, including riding.

DO YOU NEED A TRAINER?

Hiring a trainer is not a negative reflection on your own skills with the horse. It is not much different from hiring a tutor for your child, a mechanic for your car or an accountant to do your taxes. Perhaps you could have done any of these things yourself. But in hiring a professional, you are hiring someone who, because of extensive experience and education, can do the job better.

A good trainer can give your horse a refined competitive edge that you cannot. If you did have the experience and training to work the horse to that level, then you would be a trainer. The trainer has devoted his or her life to acquiring those skills, just like you have devoted yours to your profession or education.

To determine if you need a trainer, look at how you are doing with your horse now, and how you wish to do in the future. Are you competing at the level you wish to be? Are you placing fairly well? Does your horse work willingly and well? Do you feel comfortable with your horse? If you answer yes to all of those questions, you don't need a trainer.

But if you are unable to compete successfully at the level you want, then you need a trainer. He or she will help bring you up to that level by increasing your horse's skills or finding a new horse for you. That is a trainer's job. You may also want to hire a trainer if you are intimidated by or afraid of your horse. It depends on the source of your fear. If it is the horse's behavior, a trainer can help. Few horses are genuinely mean or dangerous, but many are undisciplined, mischievous or too energetic for their riders. The trainer can rid the horse of many of the behaviors you find frightening or annoying. For example, if your horse often runs away with you, the trainer can probably break him of the habit. The trainer or a riding instructor can also teach you to ride the horse better so you will be less intimidated by him.

However, the trainer cannot reshape the horse's basic personality. While he or she can teach a hot horse more constructive ways to channel the energy, the trainer cannot make a horse mellow. You will have to learn to cope with his excess energy or sell him. In some classes hot horses make the best show horses because they display a lot of flash and pizzazz, but you have to be able to handle the heat for the partnership to work. In other classes all that energy just gets in the way. The horse has to match the use he is being put to.

If you have a horse that is unmanageable for you and the trainer is unable to reconcile the two of you, sell the horse. You will both be happier if you part ways. The next person who has him may find him ideal. Another instance in which you may want to hire a trainer is to break a horse to ride. In some cases you may want to do this yourself if you are an experienced rider. But if you have a horse that seems like he will be particularly difficult, send him to a trainer. A good trainer is equipped to deal with the kind of problems the horse will present and will give the horse a good start.

. . . .
FINDING THE RIGHT TRAINER

Selecting a trainer for a show horse is much like selecting an instructor for yourself. Look for a trainer whose horses are doing well in the ring—not just the horses he or she is riding, but the ones ridden by the clients as well. How well the clients' horses are performing is a good indicator of how yours may perform. Trainers' techniques vary. If you were to take the identical horse to two different trainers, you might find that under one trainer the horse was easier for you to ride than under the other trainer. It's not that one trainer is good and the other bad. The horse might perform equally as well for each trainer. But the techniques used by one of the trainers were better suited to helping the horse perform for you than the techniques used by the other trainer.

The worth of the trainer for a horse you will ride is in how well he or she can teach the horse to perform for you. A horse that works well only for the trainer is not much use to you unless you plan to be just a spectator. If you want to show, hire a trainer who can help you and the horse work together successfully.

The trainer you select should also be skilled in the classes you want to ride. If your interest is in Western Pleasure, it does you little good to send your horse to a trainer who only does English Pleasure. Trainers often do more than one class but tend to be better in some than others.

To find a trainer, read your breed magazines and ask around among the horse community. Attend the shows at the level you wish to compete, even if you are not showing at that level yet. Show dates and places will be listed in your horse magazines. Watch the classes and talk to the people there. Ask, "If you had a horse that was good in this class, who would you take him to?" Make a list of trainers, then contact people on that list.

Which trainer you need depends on how you currently are doing in the ring. If you are doing poorly, you need a trainer whose clients are successful at the level you are at. However, if you are already placing well, hire a trainer whose clients are successfully competing at the next level up. For example, if you are doing well at small shows, pick a trainer successful at larger shows. The trainer can help pull you up there. If you pick a trainer showing at a low level, he or she can help you only as far as that level.

It's better to reach a little above where you are. I wouldn't recommend a huge leap, such as trying to hire a national-level trainer if you are still competing in small local shows, but it is good to stretch a little and hire a trainer who is working at the next showing level above yours.

Instead of starting at the very bottom and slowly working your way up through the ranks, you can start a little higher and move faster with help from the trainer and other people and resources. The work is no less hard, but you can meet many of your significant goals much faster.

Many of the people sweeping the classes at the large shows don't work much harder than those who frequent the small unrated shows. The only difference between them are their goals and the resources they have tapped into. The small shows are a lot of fun and the competitors may never have any desire to go to anything else. Or they may have tried to compete at larger shows but done poorly. It is not a reflection on them as much as on preparedness. They have not found the people, horses and educational opportunities that could bring them success at large shows.

You will create your success by utilizing the resources and help available. The resources, detailed throughout this book, include a good horse, riding instructor and trainer.

When talking to your prospective trainer, tell him or her about your goals and ask:

- *What are the trainer's qualifications?*
- *Does the trainer have any regional titles? District titles? National? World?* This will give you an idea of the trainer's scope.
- *What is the trainer's opinion of your horse?* If the trainer does not believe your horse has much potential, then you should take the horse to a different trainer. It is important that the trainer believes in the horse's abilities. However, if a number of respected horse people tell you that your horse is not going to be the kind of show horse you want, you may want to reassess your plans for him. Training only refines talent. It cannot give a horse talent that he does not already possess. If the horse cannot meet your needs, sell him.
- *If your current horse does show good potential, to what level could he successfully compete after training?* The trainer should be able to tell you roughly if the horse will be competitive at a small show, large show, regional, national or world level. The trainer may ask to keep the horse for a thirty- to sixty-day evaluation period before he or she gives you an estimation.
- *What will be done with your horse?* The trainer should be able to tell you the basic training techniques and schedule that will be followed.
- *If you need to horse shop or sell your current horse, will the trainer help you? Also, will he or she charge for the service?*
- *What will the trainer do to help you reach your goals?*
- *What are the trainer's thoughts on your needs as a rider?*
- *Who are some of the trainer's successful clients?*

- *How did he or she help them attain that success?* You may want to ask this question of some of the clients as well.
- *What fees are charged?* There will be fees for such things as training, board, grooming and perhaps hauling the horse to the shows. Ask for a detailed list of fees.
- *Does the trainer offer riding lessons? If not, what riding instructors does he or she recommend?*
- *Will the trainer go to shows and assist you if you wish?* If you are going to an important show you will want the trainer with you. At the show, the trainer may offer a variety of services, including tuning up the horse before your class and standing by the rail to offer tips as you ride by.

Look for a trainer who is skilled, patient, stable and has a good reputation in the horse community. You, the trainer and riding instructor together can formulate a plan to help you achieve success at the level you wish to show. Before committing to a trainer, inspect the trainer's facility. You want to make sure your horse will be safe and well cared for.

You also should be aware that there is a down side to hiring a trainer. There will be bills to pay, and your horse will be gone for a while. If the trainer is a considerable distance from your home, you may not get to see the horse much during the training period. That can be hard on you as a rider. Not only will you miss the horse, but your riding skills may get rusty. When you start riding again your skills will snap back into shape fairly quickly. But your first few rides after the horse's return may be discouraging. You can avoid this by riding another horse during his absence if possible.

When the horse returns, he also will feel and respond differently than before. The first time I sent a horse to a trainer I found this quite disconcerting. I had ridden the horse so long that he, in responding to me day after day, had developed a certain feel that I perceived. When you ride a horse often, you imprint on him characteristics unique to you. After the trainer works him, he will feel different. He may even feel like an entirely new horse. But he should also work better and perform at a higher level. There are some tradeoffs when you use a trainer, but if you chose the trainer wisely it can be well worth the money spent and the time missed with your horse.

. . . .

DO YOU HAVE THE RIGHT TRAINER?

The right trainer takes good care of your horse, shapes his talent to its full potential and helps you and the horse work successfully as a team. The trainer talks to you about the horse, listens to your opinions, understands what you want and keeps you up to date on his progress. He or she also uses disciplinary techniques that you agree with and that are not harsh. The quality of the trainer's work is apparent in the show ring by the many ribbons won by clients.

If this description fits your trainer, you have exactly who you need. Some trainers may fall a little short of this definition here and there, but that's all right as long as you are happy with the horse's care and the results of the training. Some trainers, for example, relate better to horses than people. That is not a major failing. But there are some areas where you cannot compromise. A talented trainer can teach your horse many good things. A bad trainer can leave him handicapped with long-term problems. Before hiring a trainer, investigate him or her thoroughly. Then after you send the horse, keep tabs on him to make sure he is progressing as he should be.

In most cases, the horse will let you know if your trainer is the right one or not. Listen closely to what his behavior and performance tell you. Is he working poorly or not progressing? This means the trainer either isn't getting the job done or is not working the horse frequently enough. Perhaps the horse consistently does poorly in the show ring. When this occurs, there are two possibilities—the horse isn't up to the level of competition, or the trainer isn't doing his or her job. If the horse seems anxious or under duress, that is another sign of problems. It may mean the horse is being pushed too hard or the learning process is being rushed.

Be particularly vigilant for signs of abuse. These include marks, swelling, welts and scrapes on the body and bruises on the gums above the upper front teeth. The horse may appear blatantly afraid or anxious around the trainer. His personality may change, such as from being a relaxed, trusting horse to one that is mean or high-strung. In his stall he may be depressed or nervous or have picked up vices such as weaving or constantly walking in circles. Even if the horse shows no signs, switch trainers if yours is fined or suspended from showing because of the abuse or drugging of another horse. The next horse could be yours. Your horse does not have the ability to protect himself from cruel or ruthless people. You must do that for him.

Also keep in mind that in cases of abuse, the American Horse Shows Association also has the authority to suspend every horse in the trainer's barn from showing, including yours. Even if the trainer has not been caught but you are certain he or she is abusing or illegally drugging a horse, remove your horse. You also should report the trainer to show authorities.

Other signs of problems with the trainer include heavy reliance on training aids that are not legal in the ring, such as chains around the pasterns or tie downs. The aids can be useful in training, depending on their application, but the horse should be able to perform well without them. Trainers who rely on aids too much sometimes are using them to compensate for lack of training time with the horse, or worse yet, lack of training ability. When you visit the horse at the trainer's, observe what kind of aids are being used and ask about their use. There may be legitimate reasons for them. However, you should also ask occasionally to see the horse worked in the kind of tack he will be shown in, minus the training aids. If he works poorly without the aids, you are not satisfied with the trainer's reasons for using them or you believe they may be hurting the horse, tell the trainer to stop their use. While you are hiring the trainer for his expertise, you have the final word in the treatment of your horse.

That extends to his care as well. While in the trainer's barn, the horse should be fed and cared for as per your instructions. A trainer who does not care for the horses well is a bad trainer and should be fired. Inadequate care is inexcusable. Your horse should be kept fit and at the proper weight. Occasionally a trainer will intentionally underfeed a horse to reduce his energy level. Whether or not this is acceptable depends on the reasons and the duration of the underfeeding. On a very limited basis, some trainers find it useful when breaking a particularly difficult horse to ride. However, over the long term, underfeeding is a sign of a lazy trainer who is using it as a substitute for sound training practices.

Another sign of a bad trainer is his or her working out of a facility that is unhealthy or dangerous. You looked at the facility before you sent the horse, but you later may notice things that weren't evident on your first visit. For example, needed repairs are not being done or the stalls are always filthy.

Your horse's health and well-being depend on your ability to assess the trainer's skills, methods and care. If you have any doubts at all, pull the horse from the facility. It is better to have no trainer than a bad trainer. Given a little time you should be able to find a good one.

In your dealings with the trainer, remember that he or she essentially is working for you. Listen to his advice and guidance, but make your own decisions. Don't be a passive client. If there is anything he is doing that you do not like or want, tell him or her. You were attracted to the trainer by his or her record and knowledge, but don't let those same qualities intimidate you into not voicing your views about what should be done with the horse. The trainer's opinions don't negate yours. Discuss with the trainer what will be done with the horse. Try to work out points where you differ. If you feel strongly about something, insist that the trainer comply with your directions. If he or she is unwilling to listen to you, you need a different trainer. As the owner, it is your responsibility and right to do what you believe is best for the horse.

GETTING THE MOST FROM PROFESSIONALS

Your relationship with trainers and instructors can have numerous benefits. They can teach you things such as conditioning, good ring positioning and how to get the best performance out of the horse. They can tell you about which shoes enhance the horse's motion and what tack works best. The grooms working in their barns can teach you about show grooming, care of the horse's coat and feeding for maximum performance.

Ask a lot of questions: How do you get the coat so shiny? Why are you using that bit? What are the benefits of using polo wraps on the front legs? How do you keep the horse from accelerating in the corners? And so on. If you don't ask, they may assume you know or may not think to tell you. You can learn a lot just by spending time at the barn watching everything that happens there, particularly the trainers working horses and the instructors giving lessons. It's like dozens of mini clinics spread out before you.

Trainers and instructors also know a vast number of other horse people. You can make connections with those people through your ties with the trainer and instructor. When you meet someone new at the barn or horse show, introduce yourself and chat with them. A lot of people come and go at the stalls of well-known trainers and instructors.

If you want to meet someone specific or visit another horse farm, the trainer or instructor can probably arrange it. Often you can do this yourself, but there are times when it helps to have someone assist you. The contacts of horse professionals can be helpful for other things as well. For example, if you are traveling to a distant horse show and need to board the horse overnight on the way, the trainer and instructor may know of farms in that area.

Your alliances with trainers and instructors can also be helpful when you are buying and selling horses—they may even offer to do most of the work for you. However, some are better at it than others, and you are your own best advocate. The professional has many horses and clients to be concerned with. You have just your own horses and can devote as much time and energy as you choose to them. You will be most successful if you use the services of professionals, but continue your own independent efforts as well. Advertise, mail out videos of your sale horses, send for videos of new horses and call about horses. My family has bought and sold many horses through the years, both inexpensive young horses and nationally known show horses. While professionals assisted in some of those purchases and sales, more than half were accomplished just through our own efforts.

There are also several instances when you should not ask your trainer and instructor to help market a horse. If you know that they dislike the horse or have a history of problems with him, it is better to do all the marketing yourself. Buyers may perceive the professionals' lack of enthusiasm about the horse. A problem also arises if the prospective buyer is one of the professionals' clients. They may discourage the sale because they don't want the horse back. Problems can also occur if the horse is extraordinary or the professionals are deeply attached to him. They may work to sell the horse—but only to their own clients. They don't want the horse to leave the barn, so they may not work very hard selling him to anyone but a client.

Marketing problems like these occur only occasionally. In general, the assistance of professionals is helpful, particularly to evaluate a horse you are considering buying.

WHAT YOU CAN DO RIGHT AWAY TO IMPROVE

- Review your needs to see if you would benefit from a trainer and/or instructor.
- Talk to knowledgeable horse people and check magazines for names of instructors and trainers. Hire the best you can find.
- Set concrete, attainable, short- and long-term goals to focus your efforts. Once you have hired an instructor and/or trainer, they can help you refine these goals. The goals should involve education, personal development, skill enhancement and accomplishments in the ring. For example, your goal over the next year might be to read five equine books, take weekly riding lessons, refine your horse's gait transitions, become better at placement and strategies in the ring, attend several large shows as a spectator and show your horse frequently, including at a show that really challenges you.

WHAT YOU CAN DO IN THE FUTURE

- Begin taking lessons as soon as possible and stick to a schedule of frequent lessons. Once in a while is not sufficient.
- After each lesson, review it mentally, visualizing yourself doing the tasks correctly. It will help you retain and more fully understand the lesson. It is also helpful to videotape your lessons, then review the tapes. It allows you to compare what you felt and did during the lesson with the quality of the performance.
- Practice on your own in between lessons. Just attending lessons is not enough to refine your skills.
- Make use of all the opportunities afforded to you by an instructor and/or trainer.

CHAPTER 3

Practicing to Win

Any time spent on a horse's back is time well spent.

In your quest for success, you will need to spend a lot of time practicing to refine your skills. How well you practice will determine in part how well you do in the ring.

The worst way to practice is to ride mindlessly around the arena without any purpose other than the need to practice. This does you little good and may even be detrimental. It bores both you and the horse. You may begin to dread practice, and the horse may become grumpy. The result may be a performance in the show ring that—while it may be technically correct— may lack spark and interest. Some of the benefits of practicing may be lost.

The key to practicing well is to keep in mind what you are working for and to never let practice become humdrum. Practicing can be challenging, interesting and even fun if you let it.

WARMING UP AND COOLING DOWN

Regardless of what you do with the horse, always warm him up before a workout and cool him out afterward. Mild exercise for ten to fifteen minutes is usually an adequate warmup, though if you are going to ask for extreme exertion he may need longer. The warmup serves a number of purposes. It helps focus his mind on work and also warms his muscles, reducing the risk of strains and injuries. As the horse works, his ability to perform well increases. Human athletes warm up before competition for the same reasons.

Cooling down the horse after exertion is also important. A horse should never be put away while he is hot. After a workout, walk the horse until the temperature of his shoulder feels normal to the touch, then keep going a little longer to make sure he really is completely cool. Do not allow him to drink or consume much food until you are certain he has cooled. This can cause serious health problems, such as colic. How long it will take to cool the horse will depend on how hot he has become and how fit he is. If the weather is cold, put a cooler blanket on him and walk him until his coat is dry to keep him from becoming chilled.

GETTING THE MOST FROM PRACTICE

Every moment you are sitting on a horse, your body is learning something. Even when you are just out on a pleasure ride your body is still tuning to the horse and absorbing lessons such as balance, timing and coordination.

Ride as often as you possibly can. Just doing a few frantic practice sessions before the big show is not enough. That is not going to net you the success you seek. There will be people in your class who have spent nearly every day of the week riding, and their work will show in their performances. If you are serious about showing, then be serious about practice. Only you can determine how much you need, but it must be frequent.

Add lots of variety to your riding sessions. The variety will keep both you and the horse interested in the workouts and prevent the two of you from getting tired of them. If the opportunity to ride other horses presents itself, ride them as well. They will widen the range of your experience and eventually help you ride your own horse better.

Because of the equine sport you have chosen, a good portion of practice will be in the arena. Since the horse is shown moving in a circle, he needs to put in some practice time in an arena, and so do you. You need to get the feel of how he moves around the space and how you can best help him negotiate the corners at every gait without changing speed or losing form. You must be able to keep yourself and the horse looking as good as possible all the way around. The corner offers the greatest opportunity for problems to be seen in both of you.

Always press the horse and yourself for the best possible on each day of practice. If you do not ask for the utmost effort now, you are unlikely to see it in the ring.

To see how well you are doing, you may find it helpful on occasion to have a knowledgeable friend watch and offer comments. It is also helpful to occasionally videotape practices. Taping offers your best chance to see how the horse and you look together. It can show you a myriad of things. It also helps you compare the things you perceived when riding with how the horse looked from the ground.

For example, when you are on the horse it can sometimes be difficult to tell just how good a head set the horse has. You learn to estimate how vertical the horse's face is set and how tall the neck is set by the feel of the horse and by glancing down at the top of the neck and head. The video can tell you how close your estimate is coming to what you want. You might find your horse is overtucked, the nose is out too far, or that he is not as elevated as you want. You can then make adjustments based on what you saw to bring him closer to the ideal.

Go into each session with a goal in mind, such as to make smoother transitions between gaits, better collect the horse, perform a really nice jog, ride more aggressively or concentrate on making your hands more still. While you will still want to practice all the gaits that will be required of you in the ring, the goal gives you a particular area to work on and try to improve. Without some kind of focus to your practices, you may find yourself mindlessly going around until you think enough time has passed for an adequate session.

Time spent in a workout is secondary to what is done in the workout. There is no set time for an effective practice session regardless of how briefly or long the clock says you have been on the horse. Different horses and riding disciplines have different needs for workout times. For some the average practice lasts an hour or more, but for others twenty minutes may be plenty. For example, a young horse or one that puts a tremendous physical effort into the practice does best with frequent but brief practices.

Concentrate during your practices on the quality rather than the time. Ignore the clock and you will usually practice the correct time for you and your horse. If the horse is working well and you have done what you wanted to accomplish, the workout can conclude. If things are going badly, continue until you feel some progress has been made before quitting.

The exception is when it is going so badly that you become angry with the horse. At that point you are more likely to lose your temper and cause a setback. It therefore is better when you become angry to conclude the workout quickly and on a positive note. Ask the horse to perform a simple task and quit after he does it adequately. You can work on the problem area another day when you are ready to be more patient. Patience is essential to successfully working with any animal.

CHALLENGING YOURSELF

In all workouts, try to add a little interest, a little challenge. A common error made in arena practice is that the rider lets the horse stay on the rail the entire time, both directions. He goes around like he is on autopilot. Not only does that nearly lull the horse to sleep, it also teaches him he should stay on the rail and just cruise around. He hardly has to pay any attention at all to you—just enough to catch the change in gaits. When you get into the ring in a crowded class, you may have problems. You will need his utmost attention and to be able to maneuver him around on and off the rail.

You need to practice more than just the gaits. Move the horse off the rail, then back onto it. Make a few rounds off the rail entirely. Do some circles. Cut across the arena occasionally. Stop the horse and make him stand quietly for a few minutes. Make a pass up the middle of the ring.

None of these moves will disrupt your goals for practice, but they will encourage the horse to listen more closely to you. They will also prepare him for some of the maneuvers he may have to make in the show ring and add some variety to the workout for both of you. If you are finding practice dull, add more of this type of thing. Play with your horse. See how subtle you can make a cue before he feels it, how slow you can make each gait and how fast you can get him to walk.

Feel the rhythms of his body. Sometime during a workout, take a break and try this exercise if you feel safe doing so: At the walk close your eyes and concentrate on the way his body moves. Feel the shifts of weight, the movements of the muscles and the fall of each hoof. Then stop him and let him stand. Keeping your eyes closed, see if you can feel his heart beating beneath you, the rise and fall of his rib cage and the gurgling in his belly. It will increase your awareness of him.

Throughout the workout try to breathe in time with the horse's movements. This is an automatic thing that riders eventually adopt, some without even realizing it. You may be doing it already. It improves timing and your overall feel for the horse. It is perhaps easiest to feel the rhythm for this at the canter or lope. Breathe out as the front leg indicating the lead hits the ground, and in as it lifts. The horse breathes the same way. At a posting trot,

You can add variety to your workouts by taking some practice sessions outside the ring. Dress safely both in and out of the arena. Whether you are riding English or western, wear a helmet, boots and close-fitting clothes.

your breathing will be timed with the post. At the slow gaits such as the walk and jog, you can breathe with each front hoof fall or pick up your normal rhythm.

Take some of your practice sessions outside of the arena (see illustration, page 39). While you do need the arena work, you don't need it all of the time. You can have a very profitable session in a field or on a trail. All of the principles you learn in the arena also work well outside of it. But if this is really going to be a practice session, approach it as such. Set your goal and do the things you would have done in the arena, even if you are working in a straight line rather than a circle.

Amid all the practicing leave a little time for play, too. Occasionally go for a pleasure ride for no other reason than to enjoy the company of the horse. Let yourself and the horse relax. Some trainers and instructors frown on taking show horses out on the trails, but I believe it provides a good break for the mind and keeps the horse happier. Even horses need a chance to relax and enjoy a quiet outing. Pleasure riding is good for most horses. The exception is a horse that finds such things traumatic, or if the trek might in some way pose a danger to the horse or rider.

Pleasure outings are as good for the rider as the horse. Though they provide a mental break, they also further your riding skills. Even when you are not paying attention, your body continues to work on learning lessons such as balance, timing and rhythm. If you do want to add in a little schooling, concentrate on keeping your hands and legs still. Your horse will appreciate it.

TRAINING AIDS

There are many types of equipment that are often used in practice but that cannot be used in the show ring. This includes tack such as draw reins, running martingales and action enhancers like weighted bell boots.

In general, there is nothing wrong with using a training aid as long as it does not hurt the horse, you understand what it does and you know how to adjust it. The aids can be helpful if used properly and detrimental if used incorrectly. A training aid is only as good as your knowledge of it.

The martingale is a good example. Adjusted properly, it is a great tool for the rider. It shifts some pressure of the bit down onto the bars of the mouth and also gives the rider more leverage to bring the horse's nose down when he is trying to evade the bit. It makes riding with a snaffle safer and teaches the horse that rooting his nose up is unacceptable. It is a commonly used piece of equipment. This type of aid, adjusted properly, can be used in every practice session without harmful side effects.

But if adjusted too long, it doesn't do its job. And when adjusted too short, it offers too much leverage and becomes a crutch for the rider in setting the horse's head. Then when the rider takes the martingale off, the head set is lost. To determine if yours is adjusted properly, pull upward on the rings. They should come up to the same level as the horse's hip bones.

Be cautious when considering using any aid that offers dramatic results, such as an instant headset or greatly improved action. Although some of these aids can be helpful, they can also cause problems if you rely on them too much.

Draw reins generally fall into this category of aids. Draw reins run from the cinch up to the bit, then to the rider's hands. When pulled back, they pull in the horse's face. They are a helpful training aid, but are easily abused.

A head set should come from you squeezing the horse forward so he meets the bit, then gives to it. Draw reins can help him learn that, but they also can teach you bad habits if you are not careful. With the draw reins, you can set the horse's head by just pulling on the reins. But that is not the correct way to get the horse to give to the bit.

In general, if you are going to use an aid that offers dramatic results, use it only occasionally rather than in every practice session. Make sure any aid you select is of genuine benefit rather than a quick fix that won't help the horse in the long run. Remember that no aid can replace good training techniques and practice time. You cannot scrimp on time with your horse, then expect an aid to make up the difference. The time invested is what really counts.

. . . .
PREVENTING BURNOUT

Burnout is a problem in any pursuit that requires dedication and persever-
ance, and showing horses is no exception. When it happens, it is one of the
true tragedies. All the years of hard work crumble away as riding becomes
an unbearable burden. It happens even to people who are at the top.

As someone who is willing to invest a large part of yourself in showing
horses, you are at risk of burning out. While it is not a greatly predictable
thing, there are some things you can do to guard yourself against it. Add a
lot of variety in practice, both in where you practice and what you are
practicing, as has been discussed.

When you feel the need, declare a horseless day, a day you will not ride.
Arrange to have no contact at all with the horses on that day. Spend the day
on something you really would like to do. Resist the temptation to waste it
on necessary but dreary tasks like scrubbing the mildew off the shower tile.
Doing such things negates the mental break you were trying to give yourself.
I find these mini-breaks quite helpful.

Burnout is also less likely to happen if you enjoy being with your horse.
That may sound oversimplistic, but affection for your horse is basic to your
ability to continue practicing and finding riding and showing enjoyable.
Affection will keep you from begrudging the horse all the time you spend
with him. Occasional bouts of resentment are normal but shouldn't last.

For a true horse person, being with a horse is an essential part of life.
There have been several periods in my life that I have been horseless, and
spent much of that time wishing I had one. I would stop on roadsides to
gaze at horses out in pastures, and linger around the fringes of shows just to
see the horses and breathe in the scents of dusty rings, wood shavings, horses
and hay.

If you care about your horse, you will want to spend time with him and
practicing will come easier to you. If you genuinely dislike your horse or
have little feeling for him, I believe it is harder to find reasons to ride on
those days when you'd really rather be doing something else.

Even very devoted people have days when they just don't feel like riding.
Some days I'd rather relax at home with the cat or go out and do something
completely nonproductive with my time. Affection for the horse can help
motivate you when you are having one of those days. My best tactic when

I'm feeling unmotivated is to think of the horse waiting for me to arrive. This works for me every time. Once I arrive, even if I initially didn't feel like riding, I still enjoy myself because I love the horse and spending time with him. Over the years I have had a few horses that I didn't like, or that didn't like me. I found working and showing them much less enjoyable.

When practicing, keep in mind that you cannot be perfect all of the time, and neither can the horse. You are going to have bad days, and so is he. Try to take them in stride. Other days will come, and you both will be better. When it's obvious either you or the horse is having one of those days, you may want to shorten your practice session or lessen the complexity of tasks you are trying to perform.

Also recognize that all learning takes time. It can be extremely frustrating when you understand how to do a task but cannot get your body to perform it properly. Be patient with yourself. You will pick it up in time and with lots of practice. Things that seem difficult now eventually will become almost automatic.

Learning takes time for the horse, too. He's not going to do everything you want instantly. You might be doing everything right, but that doesn't necessarily mean that he will. He may not understand or may not be physically able to do what you are asking. Before you punish him, be certain it is warranted. For punishment to do any good, he has to be refusing a task that he understands and is capable of doing. Give him the benefit of the doubt if it is something new and he seems to be trying hard, but doesn't quite have it right.

Always remember that showing is supposed to be fun. If you are at a show every weekend and the pace starts feeling too hectic, cut out some of the shows from your schedule. You don't have to go to every one to be successful. Just go to the ones that are particularly important and that you enjoy the most.

Try to maintain perspective at the shows. If you live and die with every victory and defeat in the ring, you are heading for trouble. No matter how good you are or how talented your horse is, there is always someone who can beat you. The best horses and riders in the world sometimes turn in bad performances. And average horses and riders sometimes shine with unexpected brilliance in the ring. I've seen riders thrown from their horses during victory laps to pick up national championship ribbons. And I've seen nationally recognized horses beaten by unknown horses that on that given day gave the best performances of their lives. Every batch of competitors brings new challenges, as does the variations in your performance and that of your horse. Keep your focus on the task at hand—riding the horse to the best of your ability. That's what you are there for, not to fret about whether you are going to win. Sometimes you will do well and sometimes you won't. That's the nature of showing.

I once had a horse that was considered practically unbeatable in the ring. Going into one regional championship, I was feeling pretty cocky since we had already beaten nearly every horse in the class before at other shows. I had also shown under the head judge before and knew he was a fan of the horse. I figured I practically had the class won before I ever even went in the gate. I should have known I was doomed to learn a lesson about sure things.

My horse, always consistent and always good, took a wrong lead, something he had never done before in a class. I was horrified. The judge was less than two yards from me at the time and just shook his head. Needless to say I did not win the title. Unexpected things happen, even when you think you have a sure thing. When you suffer a particularly bad loss, just remember that there will be other shows and other chances to excel.

THE HORSE'S VIEW

Many injuries, training problems, behavioral problems and misunderstandings occur because the rider lacks an understanding of the horse's nature. In a way, when you work with a horse you are dealing with someone from an entirely different society, with set rules and standards. In the horse's world, it is acceptable to bite, kick, shove, rear, buck and strike. This is normal horse behavior. It's how they play, socialize, protect themselves and establish who's boss.

Unless you teach the horse how he should behave toward you, he will treat you like the rest of his equine acquaintances. In the mind of the unschooled horse, he's doing nothing wrong when he bites you. He might even be playing. A horse with a dominant personality may even try to establish himself as your boss by behaving aggressively toward you.

Don't let your horse push you around or get away with actions that aren't appropriate outside of the herd. Not only could he hurt you, but his lack of good manners could also promote training problems. Teach your horse the correct way to behave toward you. You are the boss and must insist on good manners and obedience. Be consistent. Every time he behaves inappropriately, reprimand him.

Try to develop an understanding of the horse's perceptions. He sees the world much differently than you do. His hearing and sense of smell are sharper than your own. His vision in some ways is better than yours, and in other ways is worse. The horse's eyes are placed on the sides of his head, rather than in front like yours. His eye placement allows him to see in almost a complete circle around himself. But there are blind spots. A horse facing straight ahead cannot see directly behind himself or the ground directly beneath him. When you are sitting on his back, he may be able to see some of you. The horse is likely to shy when something suddenly appears out of one of these blind spots—when you walk behind him, when an object rolls under his feet, when you start to take off your coat while sitting on his back.

When you are working around areas where his vision is limited, make an extra effort to let him know what you are doing. Talk to him when you walk behind him and work around his legs. Take care when you are on his back and need to remove your coat, or reach for something such as ribbon. If you move slowly, keep hold of the reins and avoid expansive motions, you usually won't have much trouble. Moving slowly gives him a chance to notice what you are doing, so he is less likely to be startled.

The placement of the horse's eyes also affects his ability to judge dimension. You see dimensionally because your eyes are placed forward. The fields of vision of each eye overlap   in other words, the left eye sees pretty much the same thing as the right eye. The brain puts the two pictures together to form one three-dimensional image. Horses see dimension, too, but only in front of themselves. Even though they can see in almost a full circle around themselves, they have to turn their heads toward an object to see it dimensionally. Horses have such a wide field of vision that the right eye sees a largely different picture than the left. The two fields of vision only overlap in front of the horse. Where they overlap, they grant three-dimensional vision.

The clarity with which the horse sees objects is different from your own as well. Your eyes focus using muscles to change the thickness of the eye lens to focus light on the retina at the back of the eye. The brain translates that to images. It is thought that the horse's eye lacks this ability, so he uses a different technique. His eyeball is somewhat oblong, rather than round. That puts parts of the retina closer to the lens than others. Although part of the horse's environment is in focus most of the time, if he wants to see something specific he has to bring it into focus by moving his head until the image becomes sharp. You've probably seen a horse do this. When he's looking at something potentially scary, he will bob his head around as he studies it.

As the rider, it is important for you to have a basic understanding of the horse's perceptions. He is going to hear and smell things you won't, and see and interpret things differently than you would. In the ring as you move down the rail, you are seeing only about half of what he is seeing. He will see almost the entire arena and the crowd around it in a wide panorama that may contain dozens of distractions. He will see some things as three dimensional, and some things without dimension. For example, you will recognize a damp spot in the arena as nothing more than that. He may see it as just a dark patch or as a possible hole, depending on where it falls in his field of vision.

When practicing or showing, be aware of what is going on around you. Steer clear of potential problems like the damp spot, and demand that the horse's attention be focused on the task at hand. Bad behavior in the ring occurs sometimes because the horse is responding to, or being distracted by, one of the many things around him. I've seen a nationals class dissolve into mayhem over nothing more than a spot on the ground. The spot was a flickering patch of sun thrown by a roof vent into the indoor arena. A horse approaching it didn't notice it until it was almost underfoot. The horse then panicked and jumped it. The rider was nearly unseated. The horse then started bucking, the horses nearby lost their composure, and another horse coming up on the sun spot screeched to a halt and caused a pileup behind him. All of the riders caught in the mess lost their chance at a national title because of a spot on the ground. The riders could have avoided the problem had they seen the spot and steered clear of it.

Understanding the characteristics of the horse's vision also is helpful when you are pleasure riding. When riding over rough ground or obstacles, remember that the horse has to have his head at a low to moderate level and be paying attention to see the ground in front of him. If he's staring off into the distance, he's likely to do things like stumble or step into holes. For example, perhaps you are riding the horse along a trail when you encounter a small log. As he approaches it, however, he's looking at something up on the hill. Even though the log is right there in front of him, he may not have seen it well enough to step over it cleanly. Unless he puts his head down and takes a look at it, he may have difficulty telling how high he has to step to clear it. You can help him negotiate rough ground and obstacles by checking him back with the reins to get his attention, then giving him enough slack in the reins to let him move his head where needed for best vision.

The more you work with a horse and expose him to different places, the more enjoyable he will be to ride. His skills will become more refined and his performances better. As his experience widens, he will also be less likely to be distracted, become overanxious or shy. Shying and bolting are survival mechanisms. Horses evolved in the wild as grazing animals that were hunted by a wide range of predators. The horses that survived were those quick to notice anything out of the ordinary and run for their lives. Horses that were slow to shy didn't survive. Your horse may now be living in the safety of his stall or pasture, but those instincts are still strong. You can never rid him of them entirely. However, you can help him become much less flighty by working with him in as many settings as possible.

. . . .

RIDER SAFETY

Injuries can be a problem for any athlete, including you and your horse. They can quickly put an end to the show season. Some even spell the end of a horse's show career. Good riders strive to protect themselves and their horses from harm.

The majority of rider injuries are indirectly caused by the riders. They unintentionally open themselves to injury by failing to understand their horses or by trusting them too much. For example, a person who rides a horse with a halter is inviting injury. Halters are for leading, and don't allow enough control to handle a frightened or excited horse.

When you are around a horse, pay attention to him and what you are doing at all times. Remember that no horse is completely safe. Every horse, even Old Reliable, is subject to equine responses and instincts. He can become startled, kick, step on your feet, hit you in the face with his head, buck or run over you. In short, treat all horses, even your pals, with the respect they deserve.

Observe basic safety precautions. Never tie, wrap or coil anything around your hand or body when the other end is connected to a horse. When leading the horse, figure-eight the excess rope instead of coiling it. If the horse pulls back, the coil could tighten around your hand. Always behave in a calm, quiet manner around the horse. Jerky, sudden movements can startle him. Do not stand or walk directly in front of him or directly behind him, and don't sit on the ground by his feet.

Ride the horse only with tack intended for riding. Many gentle horses will let you ride them with a halter, or even a rope looped around their necks, but if problems arise you will not be able to control the horse. Both of you could become injured. When on the horse, sit facing forward with your feet in the stirrups and hands on the reins. It's fairly common to see riders with a leg looped around the saddle horn or with their legs drawn up away from the stirrups as they sit around relaxing on their horses. It's also fairly common to see bareback riders relax by sprawling out like they are taking a nap on the horses' backs. Either facing forward or backward, they rest their heads upon the horses' rumps. If the horse is startled, the rider usually falls off. It is all right to relax on a horse, but not that much. Sit on him the correct way so you don't end up lying on the ground at his feet.

When riding, dress safely by wearing clothing that fits close to your body, boots or heeled shoes (so your feet can't slip through the stirrups) and protective headgear. If you favor riding in tennis shoes, buy the tennis shoes specially made for riders. They have heels and are available through tack stores. Regular tennis shoes can slip through the stirrups and are dangerous for riding.

Many of the things it takes to be a good rider are the same as those it takes to be a safe rider. Practice hard and work on your riding and handling skills. The better you are, the less likely you are to make the kinds of errors that can lead to injuries. It also is important to understand your abilities and limitations as a rider. Overestimating your skills can lead to injury for yourself or the horse. By keeping yourself safe, you can more fully enjoy your horse and prevent the show season from being cut short by an injury.

HORSE SAFETY

Just as important as protecting yourself is protecting the horse from injury. All of your plans for the show season can end in an instant because of injury. You must make every precaution to keep your show partner from being hurt.

Injuries are caused by three things—accidents, work-related injuries and conformation that is not adequate for the task the horse is performing. In selecting your horse, hopefully you have purchased one built for the classes you are doing. That will go a long way in eliminating one cause of injuries.

You cannot eliminate accidents entirely, but by adopting some basic strategies you can reduce the likelihood they will occur. Inspect the horse trailer before each trip to make sure it remains structurally sound and that nothing sharp has come loose where the horse could be cut. Walk every foot of the horse's pasture and practice area, and inspect his stall. Remove anything in which he could become entangled or get cut. Make sure that his stall and the pasture fencing is structurally sound as well. For example, the fence should not sag or have places where he could become entangled. Fencing should also be types suitable for horses, such as board, pipe, pole or horse wire. Barbed wire can cut him badly.

There are two other hazards to a loose horse that you might not recognize—his pasture mates and his halter. Be careful about which horses you pasture your horse with. Do not put him in with a horse that is far more aggressive than he is. Most horses are fine in a herd as long as the pasture is large enough for the number of horses. However, some horses are extremely territorial and kick and bite too readily. Your horse could be injured. He could also be injured or killed if you leave the halter on him when he is loose. As unlikely as it seems, he could catch the halter on something and hang himself. Horses, like dogs, also sometimes itch their heads with a hind hoof. He could get his hoof looped through the halter.

Never, never leave the halter on. If your horse is hard to catch, feed him a snack every time you catch him. Also, catch him frequently for no other reason than to feed him. That should remedy the problem.

When you have to tie up the horse, take care. Do not tie him to anything that is not absolutely solid. Ask yourself, If he pulled back, would this move or break? The average horse weighs around a thousand pounds, a considerable amount of weight to pit against an object. You should also never leave a tied horse unattended, especially over a long period of time.

When you go riding, use a little caution. Don't ride in areas that may be dangerous to the horse or ask him to perform tasks that could lead to injury, such as cantering down a steep hill. Also avoid trotting or cantering across unknown territory unless you can see the ground clearly. The brush could be hiding holes, ditches or other hazards. There's no point in risking an injury.

One of the greatest causes of injury in athletic horses, however, is not accidents. It's physical work. Just like any other athletes who use their bodies to the fullest, horses are subject to work-related injuries to the bones, ligaments, tendons and muscles. The most common site for injuries of this type is the legs. The legs must support all of the horse's weight, drive his motion and help diffuse the concussion of the hoofs striking the ground. The horse also has no muscles in the leg below the knee, just tendons and ligaments.

Most leg injuries are minor strains that can be remedied by laying the horse off for a few days. But some injuries are serious, involving torn tissues or fractured bones. They take a long time to heal. Some are so serious the horse is never again able to perform.

To help prevent injuries of all kinds, know the capabilities of your horse and do not try to push him beyond them. When your horse becomes tired, end the practice session. Fatigue is one of the main causes of injury. Keep in mind that horses differ in the amount of work they can do before becoming seriously fatigued. Young horses cannot do as much as mature horses, and flabby horses cannot handle as much as fit horses. Good practice techniques require that you ride frequently. You cannot substitute one marathon session for lots of shorter ones and expect good results. Horses learn best through repetition. Frequent practice also helps keep the horse in condition. There is no greater thing you can do to prevent injuries than to keep the horse in good shape.

In practice sessions, protect the horse's legs by not riding him on ground that is deep, slick or hard. In general, if you can hear the hoof echoing off the ground, it's too hard. If you feel the horse picking his feet up higher than usual or struggling to make it across the ground, the footing is too deep. If the horse slips, the ground is too slick.

To ward off strains, warm up the horse before asking for tasks that take great exertion. You may also want to consider protective leg gear for your horse, such as splint boots or polo wraps. Splint boots cover the front legs from knee to pastern and give the horse extra support there. Polo wraps cover the same area. The principle is similar to human athletes wrapping their legs, wrists or knees. There are many kinds of protective leg gear for many different purposes. Splint boots, or other gear that protect the same area of the leg, are good basic leg protection used by most breeds and sports.

In some cases you may need to take precautions against injury for horses turned loose as well. Take care when turning a horse out to romp in the pasture after he has been stall confined. It is great for him to get out and play as long as he doesn't play so hard he hurts himself. If you are turning him out daily, give him at least a few hours outside every time. Horses turned out only for very short periods tend to run themselves to near exhaustion the entire time out, because the time is so limited. If you are turning out an extremely high-strung horse that has been confined for many days in a stall, you may even want to consider lunging him first to take the edge off. It sounds excessive, but when penned-up energy is combined with the excitement of being outside, a horse can push himself so hard in the first few minutes out that he hurts himself.

In addition to protecting your horse from injury, you also need to guard against illness. A show horse travels to many places and is exposed to many horses and situations. The stress of the show may also lower his resistance to illness. Keep his vaccination and worming schedule current. Consult your veterinarian about what vaccinations are needed and when. Remember to tell him or her about the places you typically show the horse. Those areas may have diseases that are not common in yours. The horse may need a wider range of vaccinations than had he stayed at home.

WHAT YOU CAN DO RIGHT AWAY TO IMPROVE

- Begin setting goals for your practices.
- Add more variety both in what you do during sessions and where you have sessions.
- Take a look at any training aids you may be using to ensure that they are correctly adjusted and being used properly.

- Ride with safety in mind. Wear heeled boots, a practice helmet (bicycle helmets work well, too) and close-fitting clothes. Put protective leg gear such as polo wraps on your horse's legs, and avoid riding him in risky areas. Protect the horse from injury by riding sensibly and inspecting his trailer, pasture and stall for hazards.

WHAT YOU CAN DO IN THE FUTURE

- Practice as often as you can. A few practices right before the show are not enough if you are serious about showing.
- Explore some new places to pleasure ride, and try to find an indoor arena where you can ride when the weather is bad. You may want to board your horse there in the winter, or make arrangements to use the ring if you have the ability to haul the horse back and forth easily for practice sessions.
- Keep the horse in condition to improve his performances and protect him from injury.
- With help from your veterinarian, establish a worming and vaccination schedule to guard against illnesses.
- Look for educational opportunities such as clinics, instructional videotapes and reading. Obtain a book on horse perceptions from your local library or bookstore.
- Give yourself a horseless day now and then when you start feeling ragged.

Are You Ready to Advance?

Before you become a great rider, you have to have the courage to be bad.
Everyone rides badly the first time. He or she also rides badly the second
time, and the third, and so on until slowly competence emerges, and then
skill and then a feel for the art. The same is true of showing. Everyone who
starts showing makes a lot of errors and earns a lot of low placings. A rider
must attend many shows and enter many classes before he or she develops
good show ring skills and strategies and performs consistently.

In riding, there aren't any "overnight successes." Everyone who stands in
a winner's circle has earned the right to be there. It's wonderful if you are
blessed with a natural aptitude for riding, but it is not the end of your horse
career if you are not. It just means you will have to work harder. There is
no substitute for numerous hours spent on horseback and a passion to learn.
Learning to ride well and be successful in the ring takes time. It also takes
a willingness to continue even when you know you are not riding as well as

some of the people around you. But each time you get on the horse you get slightly better. Think back on your skills when you started riding and you will realize how far you have come already.

You should not wait until you are an adept rider to enter a show or to attempt to compete at a larger show than you usually enter. Part of the education of a winning rider comes from things learned while in the show ring. Don't deprive yourself of that. Showing will also increase your motivation by giving you short-term goals to focus on. For example, perhaps in five years you want to be showing at a regional level. That's a good goal, but a very distant one in relation to your day-to-day practices. You would practice more often and become closer to your big goal if you had lots of little goals along the way. Take the plunge and go to the shows. As you improve, you can advance to increasingly higher levels of showing.

YOUR FIRST SHOWS

You are ready to enter a show when you are comfortable with the horse, confident in your ability to control him and he is performing his gaits and obeying your requests with reasonably good accuracy. His performance must meet the basic standards of the class in which you wish to show him. For example, if you want to show him in Western Pleasure, he must be jogging and loping slowly. Before you enter a show, you should also watch at least one horse show and see what will be expected of you.

Don't decline entering a show out of fear of how you will look, how the horse will look, how you will do or because you don't know how to enter. The uncertainty you feel early in your show career is natural. When you arrive at a show, the nervousness can become almost overwhelming. All your competitors may seem to look so good and so self-assured and have such nice horses. Don't worry about them. They have already gone through the same feelings you are now having. When you look at them, you are just seeing what you will look like with a little more experience. Just do the best you can and you'll be fine. Your placings will probably start out low, but will improve over time. It is also likely your placings will be inconsistent as well. You may place well in one class, then in a short period of time go in another class and place badly. This situation is fairly common with beginners, because their performances sometimes vary greatly from one class to the next.

You can help prepare yourself for the ring and quell some of the nervousness by doing your homework about showing. Attend some shows as a spectator first. At the show you will see everything that is expected of you in appearance and performance. To do well, you need to see what others are doing to win. When you start feeling nervous, assure yourself that you have been practicing hard and you can show your horse well. The riders in that show ring aren't doing anything different from what you have done at home in practice. You don't have to be perfect. Have the courage to try. You may be better than you think.

Having the courage to try also means not letting yourself get discouraged if a show goes badly. Everyone has bad shows. Everyone has been to at least a few shows where he or she never won a ribbon, the performances went badly or the horse went lame. Those kinds of shows happen. But so do the shows that are wonderful and exciting and successful. Just look upon the bad shows as experiences that may help you do better in the future. Be persistent in your efforts to win show ring success.

Show entries for the smaller events can often be picked up in your area tack stores. Larger shows across the country are listed in breed publications and in the American Horse Shows Association magazine that comes to all AHSA members. The listings give you phone numbers and places to write to get entry forms.

The entry form comes in a premium book or with a few pages attached that explain all the classes, fees and rules. On the form is the phone number of the show secretary, who can answer any questions you may have about the show or filling out the form. Though you can probably fill out the form competently on your own, it is nice to have the advice of an experienced horse person to guide you the first few times. He or she can also make suggestions about what classes you may want to enter.

Entry forms at small, unrated shows are fairly simple and vary little from show to show. Entry forms at large shows are fairly detailed but also vary little from show to show. Once you know how to fill out a form, you can fill out any form at that level of show. The show structures are also similar. Once you have been to one show, you know the basic workings of all shows at that level.

ADVANCING TO BIG SHOWS

You are ready to advance to a higher level of competition when you are consistently placing in the top three. This may be in all of your classes at the shows or in one specific class. Placing consistently high in a specific class is an indication you could be showing at a higher level in that one class. It also is an indication that if you dropped some of the other classes and concentrated more on training and showing in that one, you and the horse might be able to really excel.

When selecting shows at which to ride, consider your skill level and that of the horse. Can you be competitive at this show? It is demoralizing to go to a show where you are so overmatched you have only a slim chance of seeing even the lowest-place ribbon. Losing repeatedly may increase your awareness of how much more you need to practice, but losing too much can make you wonder why you even try.

At the same time, you should pick shows that challenge you and the horse. That's how you grow and improve. Winning every class is pointless if there is no competition. It may sound like fun, but it is a useless exercise. You might as well buy trophies for all the good it does you. Challenge yourself. Attend shows that give you some chance of success, but do not guarantee it.

It's natural to feel a little uncertainty when going to a larger show than you are accustomed to attending. I had been riding for years before I attended my first genuinely large show. I couldn't have been more nervous had it been my first time in the ring. All of my competitors looked so good, and I felt out of place and inadequate. But those feelings are based more on nervousness than lack of equine skills. Don't let your doubts get in the way of your desire to show at larger events. Before you venture into higher realms of showing, go on a fact-finding mission just as you would have if this was your first show. To show on a higher level, you should first know what the higher level is.

You need to see how things work, note the quality of horses and riders there, learn the interpretation of various styles of riding and dress, and have a chance to absorb the feel of the show. Roam the grounds, talk to people, watch the classes and soak it all in. When the time comes that you think you are ready to attend such a show, this kind of homework will help you be prepared for the adventure ahead. It also will help you fit in with the other competitors.

Among the more common errors made by people new to showing or who are showing at a higher level for the first time are:

- The rider lacks information about what is required at that level.
- The rider doesn't notice the qualities of the horses and riders who win.
- The horse and rider are not yet ready to be at this kind of show.
- The trainer or instructor assisting the rider is not qualified for this level.
- The horse's grooming does not conform with that of the horses showing successfully.
- The horse's tack does not conform or does not fit properly.
- The horse's training is not adequate for the level of show he is attending. When the training isn't sufficient, the performances are poor.
- The horse is out of shape, fat or skinny. Fit horses perform better than those that are not.
- The rider doesn't warm up the horse properly for the ring. Usually the rider either does not warm him up enough, or rides him so long that he is overly tired for his classes.
- The rider's dress is rumpled, unpolished or deviates too far from the style of the show ring.
- The rider shows a lack of finesse in handling and riding the horse, such as by leaning way forward to cue for the canter, or using expansive hand motions to steer the horse.

You can avoid many of these mistakes by following the examples set by winning riders. Go to the big shows and see the level of competition you are shooting for. If you have questions, follow a competitor back to his or her stalls and ask. Immediately after the class the rider will be tending to the horse, but if you wait around a little while by the stalls you will get your chance.

You may also find it interesting to chat with the people sitting next to you in the show audience. Since most of the people there are connected to the show, you have a fairly good chance of being by people who have been showing a while. Ask them how long they've been showing, and any other questions that come to mind, such as "Why did that horse win over this one?" Not everyone there is going to be an expert, but you could learn something interesting.

The show is also the place where you can see if your trainer and riding instructor are up to par, as has already been discussed. If they have horses and students successfully competing at this level, the level you want to be at, then you have chosen wisely. If not, you may want to make a change. People operating at a low level of showing cannot boost you to a high level.

People who try to compete at a big show without ever having seen one run a high risk of going home disappointed. Either their skill level is not high enough yet or they just didn't know to do some of the small things that would have helped their placing. They work very hard, but because they have never actually seen such competition they may be working on the wrong things or be missing something vital. It's like trying to write a book report when all you have read is the synopsis on the jacket. It will be lacking in detail and not reveal all the things that were important.

Also running the risk of disappointment are those who may go to watch the shows, but do not keep an open mind about what they see. They simply go on believing their horses are better and perform better than anyone else's possibly could. When they begin showing and place poorly, they may blame it on bad judging, or something ludicrous such as the judge hating the color of the rider's shirt. This is called barn blindness.

It works the other way as well. Some people think their horses could never measure up to those they see in the ring. Their horses may be quite good, but they will never see the inside of the ring because the owners are too intimidated to try. It is easy to be intimidated when you start comparing your horse at home with those you see at these shows. But it isn't a fair comparison. You are seeing the show horses at their very best. They are conditioned, trained and have undergone a great deal of grooming. They are, in a way, like movie stars or magazine models—the natural beauty and talent are clear, but they are also being highly enhanced. Part of what you are seeing is glamour and illusion. If all goes well for the riders, you will only see what the riders want you to see.

On the other hand, you have seen both the worst and best of your own horse. You've seen him at his fuzziest, dirtiest and naughtiest. You know everything he is capable of. The thing to remember is that those horses you see in the ring have the same flaws. When the glamour of the ring is gone, they can be just as fuzzy, dirty and naughty as your horse. You would be amazed if you could see what the same horses look like in the dead of winter. Even national and world champions roll in the dirt, get manure stains on the sides of their heads and grow shaggy hair. I've seen a number of nationally renowned show horses that during the shaggy off-season were almost unrecognizable from their show images—my own horses included.

The other side of this is that when you take your horse in the ring, the judges see the same polish and glamour in your horse as they saw in the others. When your horse is groomed and well trained, he can look just as good as the other horses do.

When you are attending these high-level shows, try to be objective. Don't blind yourself with thoughts of your horse's supreme greatness or terrible weaknesses. Really look at the horses being shown and the people showing them. Learn something from them so that when you challenge them in the ring, you know what you are doing and are ready to be there. There is much more to a class than walk, trot and canter. You need to know what will be expected of you besides the obvious.

Say Western Pleasure is your passion. Among the things you might notice in your observations at the big shows is that the western jog is slower than what you have been asking of your horse. Or that the noses of the horses are tucked in a little further. Or that dark felt saddle pads are in wide use, but yours is a big, fuzzy, orange one. Or that everyone is wearing gloves.

You will see a whole range of things like this, some minor and others significant, that you can adjust to fit showing at that level. Had you not made this effort, you may have come to the show gloveless, riding a horse that jogged too fast and stuck his nose out too far and had a big, fuzzy pad. The gloves and pad would not significantly impact your placing, other than suggesting to veteran show people that you might be new. The horse's jog and improper nose placement, however, would have damaged your placing and perhaps dropped you out of the ribbons altogether.

The first time I went to a big show, my family just loaded up the horse and off we went without doing hardly any homework on that level of showing. I might as well have posted a sign on my back that said "I have no clue what I'm doing." Though I placed in a few classes, I did not do well, in part because I knew nothing about the show, the level of competition, what was expected of me or how I should have groomed myself and the horse for this kind of competition. I did things such as ride an English Pleasure class huntseat when everyone else was riding saddleseat. My grooming efforts weren't much better. Although I had gotten fancy and was using clippers instead of scissors to do the bridle path, I was still using cornstarch to try to make the horse's socks white. Sometimes I put on so much that little white clouds puffed off his legs when he walked. That's definitely not high-level grooming.

When you go to these shows, look long and hard at what people in your class are doing and how they appear. Everything they do is for a reason. They are conforming in their appearance and the performance of their horses to a standard that exists at that level of competition. You want your horse to perform like the winning horses perform. And you want your physical appearance to be just as polished and sharp as that of the winners.

When watching the top horses and riders, pay particular attention to things such as the qualities of the horses' performance. How fast or slow are the horses' gaits? Is the motion of each horse fluid or animated? Is there lots of flex to the knee or hardly any? Are the strides long, or short and choppy? And so on. Watch the motion of the hind legs as well as the front. Also note the horses' bearing and presence. Do their bodies look compact or long? Do they seem mellow or energetic? How high or low are the necks set and how deeply are the heads tucked?

Look at the specific types of tack the horses are wearing. Notice things such as the type of bit and headstall, the pad worn, the saddle used, the kind and color of girth and how it is all adjusted. Also look at the riders' dress, including types of attire, colors, fit and what makes it appealing. Notice, too, the riders' overall bearing and manner, how they sit and cue the horse, and other features such as makeup, facial expressions, how they have done their hair, if they have a flower in their lapels, etc.

Note how the horses are groomed as well. This would include what areas have been clipped, if the mane or tail is braided, where oil or dressing has obviously been applied and so on.

This will provide you with insight into the qualities of winning horses and riders at that level. Compare what you see to what you are doing. What do you admire about the successful people in the ring? In what ways are you doing as well as they are? Where are you falling short? What adjustments could you make to improve your own performance and appearance? Make mental notes on the areas on which you need to work.

At the shows, it is also good to make an effort to go to the parties and other social events. They are not only fun, but are a good place to meet and talk with other horse people. Everything you learn puts you one step closer to your goals. As you continue in your quest for success, the shows you attend will get larger and larger until you are where you want to be.

WHAT YOU CAN DO RIGHT AWAY TO IMPROVE

- Get a listing of large and small shows near you, either from the American Horse Shows Association magazine, a breed magazine, tack store or someone you know showing at that level.
- Begin attending larger shows as a spectator. Make note of the traits of the winning horses and riders at shows you attend, and compare them to your own traits.

WHAT YOU CAN DO IN THE FUTURE

- Ride in your first show, if you have never shown before.
- If you are an experienced rider, compete at one or more shows that will really challenge you and the horse, but that offer some chance at success.
- Work toward improving those areas where you believe you and the horse fall short of those winning qualities.

CHAPTER 5

The Winning Look

Success in the show ring revolves around appearances as well as talent.

Image is a big part of showing. Judging is a visual art of quick decisions made by comparing one horse and rider to another,

To do well, especially at large shows, you and the horse at least should look like you have the possibility of winning. If you do not, you are asking the judge to overlook your sloppiness, and there·is no reason for that. You want to attract his or her eye favorably. Some judges in large classes will make the decision whether or not to watch you within the first few instants of the class. Fail to impress the judge in that time and you become one of the many who leave without a ribbon.

An experienced horse person, seeing a group of riders waiting to enter a class, can often tell roughly who in the class will do well and who will get the gate. There are a number of reasons for this. Successful riders take on an increasingly professional and polished look. All the time spent around horse shows and working with horses becomes visible in a myriad of ways, including how the horse and rider are groomed. The rider also exudes an air of confidence, skill and ease in handling the horse. The horse is likely to be of high quality as well, since good riders seek out good horses. The combination of fine appearance, confidence, skill and quality creates a winning look.

The riders who habitually do poorly rarely have the same look. They may have worked very hard, but there are gaps. The first may be the horse or the

Pretend you are a judge walking down this line of riders. Which rider looks like a winner? To be successful, you have to look successful. Number six looks the part because her appearance is tidy, well prepared and professional. Her clothes are current, clean and well fitted. The horse is nicely groomed. Number three, on the other hand, has an appearance that says she cares little about the class. The horse is dirty. The rider's clothes are rumpled, poorly fitted and grimy. The hat is battered and the number is crooked. The last rider is tidy, but conveys the impression that she does not know what is desired in the ring. Her clothes and the saddle pad do not conform with what is commonly being used. And the braid makes it hard for the judge to see her number.

training of the horse. Even with that aside, there are often other elements that detract from the horse and rider's look. There are just as many things that can make you look bad as can make you look good. At the very least you want to look appropriately prepared and dressed for the ring (see illustration, page 63).

A sharp riding outfit, appropriate tack and well-groomed horse are not going to win the class for you. It takes a whole lot more than that. But it does send a message to the judge and your competitors that you are serious and competent. Looking sharp will also help your confidence. In the ring, that confidence can help you give a better performance.

TACK

Start evaluating your show ring appearance by looking at the tack. Piece by piece, go through the tack. Is it clean and in good condition? Is it correct for the class? Is it of the type being used in the ring today? Does it fit you and the horse well? Does the pad fit the saddle and the horse? Does the color of the leather or the saddle blanket look nice with your clothes and the horse? Light-colored leather looks terrible on some horses, as do some colors of pads.

The tack says a lot about your knowledge of horses. Going in to the ring with a crooked saddle pad or browband conveys the image that you are sloppy. A caveson set low and loose on the horse's nose says you don't really know what it is for. Tack that is too small or too large may give the impression that you borrowed it at the last minute and are not serious about showing. Tack that is inappropriate for the class says you are not very interested in the class. Dirty tack makes it appear you put little effort in preparation.

Make sure your tack is clean and fits. Within the limits of your budget conform to what is being used in your classes of interest. For example, in most higher-level shows using colorful web tack is considered in extremely bad taste. Know what is appropriate for your circumstances. Some tack use regulations will be in the AHSA rule book or the rule book for your breed, or will be listed under horse show regulations in the premium book.

But some guides are unwritten, a matter of what is considered acceptable rather than what is required. The unwritten rules you learn mostly through observation. If at show after show you look at your competitors and notice you are the only one using or not using something, you may want to consider making a change.

. . . .
CLOTHING

The criteria you can use in evaluating your clothing is quite similar to what you use with tack. Is the clothing clean and in good condition? Does it fit properly? Do the colors look good on you and on the horse? Is the style current with what is being worn in the ring? If your clothing passes all the tests, you've got a good outfit.

Your outfit does not affect your performance but it does affect the overall impression you make. It therefore can affect your placing. For example, if your clothing has elements that flop—such as an overly bulky shirt or long fringe—it will make your horse's motion look rougher than it is. That can damage your placing in a pleasure class, since pleasure horses are supposed to be smooth. A truly bad outfit can also take away from your overall appearance and that of the horse. He cannot look sleek and well groomed if you do not.

Clothing that is too small or poorly fitted can make you look gangly, sloppy and amateurish. By obscuring the lines of your body, it can also make it appear that you have poor riding posture. Make your clothing work for you. With the right fit, style and choice of colors you can emphasize your best qualities and shadow areas where you are weak.

If your present outfit doesn't look as sharp or professional as you would like, try to isolate what gives it that look. Small problems such as a shirt that is too baggy can be fixed with a trip to a local seamstress or tailor. Dull-looking boots can be polished. A color or two can be removed or changed by replacing one of the elements, like the pants. Sometimes an outfit that combines too many colors, or combines colors that do not really look good together, takes on a tacky look. Removing or replacing a color can improve it substantially.

If you can't isolate the problem, the whole outfit may need replacing. Pattern your clothing after that worn by successful competitors. That doesn't mean you need to copy them exactly. You are an individual with individual tastes. Your outfit will show that individuality. What you will copy is how your competitors are achieving a polished, competent look with their clothes. In other words, look at what types of clothes are worn—shirt, vest, tie, pants, boots, jacket, etc. Then note the styles of each and how they fit.

Choose clothes that are in line with show regulations, and that fit like they were tailor made for you even if they were not. They should be clean and well pressed, and not rumpled or baggy. Nothing on them should flop or sag. The sleeves and pant legs should be long enough that the clothes look like they were meant for you, not a much shorter person. And remember that they must fit you correctly *while you are on the horse*. A sleeve or pant leg that is barely long enough in the dressing room will become too short when you get on the horse. Remember that you ride with arms and legs bent. When trying on clothes, bow your legs wide, crouch a little and bend your arms like they would be when you are riding. If the sleeves and pant legs still are long enough, they will be so when you are riding.

While your budget for clothes may limit your options, it does not take money to look clean, neat and tidy. You may want to ask someone current with what is being worn in the ring to help you select the right riding wear. The people who specialize in selling riding clothes can also be quite helpful in getting the right fit, fashion and selection of colors.

When you are putting together an outfit, put lots of care and consideration into picking the color. Color has a tremendous impact on how you and the horse look together.

Color can enhance, dampen or pick up odd hues in the horse's coat. It also can make you look pale or tanned, fat or thin, outrageous or conservative. It can even emphasize or hide body movement as you ride. The color should be tasteful, and complement your complexion and your horse's coat. Don't just pick your favorite color. It might look ghastly with your horse or be inappropriate for the show ring.

Tastefulness and tidiness are the most important considerations. Keep them in mind in any clothing selection.

Following that, select colors that look good on the horse. Hold the color up to him and notice how it blends with his coat. Also note any hues it emphasizes in the coat. The color you wear has a greater impact on the appearance of his coat than you may realize. You can make his color look rich or dingy. For example, when I was riding a dappled gray, I had three riding coats to choose from—one light blue, one tan and one a silk burgundy. The blue coat make the white in the dapples look very white, and the gray a sterling gray. The tan coat produced a ghastly effect, as if dirty water had spilled across him. His nice gray dapples seemed to turn brown. The burgundy coat gave his color a warm, rich look without fading his dapples to brown. I used the blue and the burgundy in the ring.

The burgundy was my favorite on him because it fit his aggressive personality and it was beautiful. The color seemed to reflect down into his coat. It emphasized that he and I were a team. Riding is about the horse and rider becoming one being. You can increase the appearance of oneness with your horse through the colors you choose. Dance partners do the same thing by wearing outfits that echo each other's colors. Poorly chosen colors, on the other hand, make it appear that you are just sitting there on top of the horse and are not in tune with him.

Before choosing an outfit, always hold the color up to the horse's coat, if possible. Some riding clothing makers offer fabric samples to make this easier. At the very least take a good photo of your horse clothes-shopping with you. Sometimes colors you think will look good, don't.

The color you choose should also look good on you. Hold it up to your face and note the effect. Does the color accentuate your complexion or deter from it? Different colors affect various skin tones in various ways. A color can enhance the color of your eyes and the healthy tones in your skin, or wash out your face and make you look pale. Some colors can even make you look gray or greenish.

You may already know what the best colors are for you. Look in your closet. Of the outfits you have, which ones look best on you? What colors are they?

Remember when selecting an outfit that you are dressing to be seen from a distance rather than up close. It is the judge you are trying to impress, and he or she sees you mostly from yards away. Any pattern you choose should look good from a distance. Also remember that brighter colors draw attention. That is a good thing if you want that scrutiny, but bad if you are not up to it. For example, it would be a mistake to wear bright or white gloves unless your hands are extremely still. Darker colors will help you hide such flaws. When you are a topnotch rider you can wear any color you please within the limits of show etiquette. But on your way to becoming that rider you may want to choose subdued colors to help camouflage your weak areas. Darker colors and vertical lines can also help you appear more slender. If you are heavy, avoid big patterns.

To help your budget, chose a versatile color for your pants, chaps or jodhpurs so they will go with many other colors. For example, let's say you're putting together a western outfit and are trying to pick a color. The chaps are probably one of the more expensive parts of your outfit and you're not going to want to buy another pair soon. But it's nice to have some variety in the outfits you wear. What you need is a chap color that will look good with many different colors. This will allow you to change your look by changing the shirt you wear with the chaps, rather than having to build a whole new outfit with new chaps. Selecting a basic color for your chaps such as navy blue, black, dark brown, dark burgundy or dark green will give you that leeway. The darker shades will hide some leg movement as well. The colors also look good with most colors of horse, with the exception of the brown. Brown makes some shades of gray horses look dingy.

In the shirt you add to the outfit, you can look conservative with a dark coordinating color, tall and slim with vertical lines, bold with a bright color or lively pattern, or softer with a pastel. If you don't like dark colors for your legs, you can put bold or soft colors there as well, but try to stick to colors that go with many other colors. I once picked a nice shade of turquoise for my chaps, then spent nearly the whole show season trying to find a shirt to go with them. The only thing that seemed to work with them was a white and black. So much for wardrobe versatility.

For your hat, match the color of your chaps. It ties your outfit together. It also helps with the outfit's versatility, since anything that matches the chaps will match the hat.

If you are riding hunt seat or show hack, you don't have much leeway in clothing colors. Follow the conservative rules of dress for your class.

In saddleseat, some breeds allows bright coats, but others prefer conservative colors, accept the bright colors only on women or only allow bright colors during day classes. Read your rule books to find out what is acceptable. If yours is a breed that uses the colorful coats, you can follow the same basic principles as with the chaps above. Go with dark, versatile colors on your jodhpurs and change your look by wearing different coats or vests with them. Match your hat to the jodhpurs.

. . . .

HATS

To add to your crisp look, have your western and soft English hats blocked regularly. A droopy hat or one that is too big for your head detracts from your image. Also keep in mind that light-colored and white hats tend to make you look taller. That's fine if you are on a large horse, but if your horse is small you may want to avoid light hats. When you appear taller, the horse appears smaller.

. . . .

HAIR AND MAKEUP

Putting up hair is probably my most hated pre-class activity. I was never meant to be a hairdresser. But like every other element of appearance, what is done with the hair is important. It must look tidy and professional.

Nice, short hair is the easiest and always looks nice. All you have to do is put on your hat. The shorter the short hair, the better. Mid-length and long hair is a little more difficult. Regardless of your sex, don't let it straggle out under the hat. Tie it up under your hat, or if you are female pull it back into a bun. If your hair is long enough to need confining but too short to make a bun, you might want to attach a bun of false hair. Tidy is the key word here. Whatever you do with it, put enough hair dressing and spray on it to keep little strands from wisping out.

Avoid long ponytails, braids and anything that flops. The flopping can make your horse look rough to ride. The length also can obscure the judge's view of the number on your back.

If you lack hair skills like I do, grab up your hat, go down to the local hairdresser and have him or her teach you quick ways to do your hair for the ring.

If you wear makeup, use colors that are a little more bright than usual for you. Remember, you will be seen mostly at a distance. Putting on makeup for a show is somewhat like putting on makeup for a play. It needs to be a little heavier and more intense, but not gaudy or in bad taste. After you put it on, back up a way from the mirror and see how you look.

Also keep in mind how the ring will affect your appearance. I get quite pale. Some people flush red. You can compensate somewhat for these color changes with the makeup. Use brands that won't wash off easily or you will sweat them off.

. . . .

THE LOOK OF CONFIDENCE

Confidence is your ally in the ring. It enhances your riding skills and projects the image to the judge that you are the one to watch.

Confidence in the ring is something that comes with time and experience. But you can help develop your ring presence by patterning your attitude

A confident look makes all the difference. A confident rider keeps eyes and chin up, shoulders back, body erect but relaxed, and handles the horse with ease.

after that of confident riders. You can also work to avoid displaying the characteristics of the nervous, uncertain rider. Just as confidence is apparent, so is uncertainty. The uncertain rider often shows his or her lack of confidence in the set of the body, the expression on the face and the handling of the horse. This can be detrimental to placings both in pleasure and equitation classes. While the confident rider is telling the judge that he or she is a contender, the uncertain rider is telling the judge that he or she is having trouble (see illustrations, page 70 and below).

The confident rider keeps his or her eyes up and looking ahead. He or she watches for openings on the rail and avoids crowds of horses. He or she glances down only occasionally to check the horse. The timid rider looks down almost all the time, and cannot see what is coming up ahead. Often his or her placement on the rail is more by accident than design.

The confident rider's facial expression may show intense concentration but no nervousness or fear. He or she may even look a little cocky. The unconfi-

This exaggerated look betrays the rider's nervousness, uncertainty and timidity. The unconfident rider usually looks down and wears a tense expression. His or her body often looks slightly curled, with the hands drawn close to the body and shoulders slumped. The rider may struggle to handle the horse, and the horse reflects the rider's nervousness.

dent rider often looks tense, uncertain and sometimes scared. If he or she tries to wear a smile through the class it is likely to look strained or become a grimace.

The confident rider's posture is erect but relaxed. The unconfident rider often slumps forward as a result of having dropped his or her eyes. This rider may also look slightly curled, with the arms pulled close to the body and the legs drawn upward.

The confident rider handles the horse with an easy manner and has complete control. If the horse does act up, the rider handles the situation calmly. The unconfident rider may exaggerate cues or struggle with the horse. He or she may not have complete control all of the time. If the horse acts up, the uncertain rider see it as a disaster and may panic.

The confident rider is aggressive in the ring. The uncertain rider is timid and slow to react.

The confident rider's horse reflects the rider's confidence. The uncertain rider's horse reflects the rider's uncertainty.

By studying the characteristics of confident riders, you can improve your placings. Even if you are a little uncertain, it does not have to show. Work to rid yourself of the characteristics of an uncertain rider and adopt a more confident image.

. . . .
PHYSICAL ADVANTAGES

To look good and do well in the ring, you also need to take good care of yourself. Keep your weight at a reasonable amount for someone your size and exercise to keep your body strong. Eat nutritious food, avoid things that aren't good for you and in general try to lead a healthy life. You are an athlete. Treat yourself like one.

. . . .

THE HORSE'S APPEARANCE

Grooming the horse is the last step in a process that creates a polished look in the show ring. Part of what makes a horse beautiful comes from genetics, but the rest comes from you. Beauty is increased by good care and conditioning that is accented by skilled grooming.

Nutrition

At its most basic, feeding a horse is largely a matter of giving him high-quality feed in an amount that matches his size and activity.

A horse that receives poor quality food or not enough of it will have a low energy level, plodding attitude and a coarse, dull coat. He may look thin with his ribs standing out, or be oddly proportioned with a big belly but bony shoulders and hind quarters. It is not just the fat that is missing. He lacks muscle as well. Not only will he look bad, but his athletic skills will be hampered by his low energy and overall poor condition.

A similar thing occurs if you let him become obese. While he may be healthier than a starving horse, the fat is a burden to his body. His heart and lungs must work harder, and the extra weight increases the concussion on his legs. He will not be able to turn in as good a performance as a horse that is fit. When you are competing in a large show you will be in classes full of horses in top shape. Make sure yours is one of them.

Your horse will tell you if you are feeding him too much or too little. Just look at him. Feed too much and his neck will become thicker and his belly and rump will become rounder. If you press on him, the flesh will feel squishy. That is an indication you should cut back on his feed.

If you can just barely see his ribs and feel them as you run your fingers along his barrel, his weight is fine. It is normal to see ribs. It is also better for the horse to be a little thin than fat. Young horses in particular tend to stay a bit thin until they stop growing at age five or six. It's nothing to worry about.

On the other hand, if the ribs are standing out in deep relief, he is too thin. Increase his feed gradually, using mostly hay. Too much grain can cause problems, especially in growing horses.

Use hay to fuel his basic needs and grain for extra energy. A mature horse that is not being worked does not need grain unless she is pregnant. Good-quality hay that is green, good smelling, clean and leafy is all he needs. A standard rule is to feed around one and a half to two pounds of hay for every hundred pounds the horse weighs.

Add grain when you start working him. For a medium-size horse of around a thousand pounds, two pounds of a grain such as oats or barley for every hour worked is a nice conservative amount. The horse will need more if workouts are high intensity or if she is pregnant. A feeding guide or veterinarian can help you determine how much your specific horse needs.

Most owners of performance horses also add vitamins and minerals to the diet. If you choose to feed a supplement, have your veterinarian recommend a good brand. Follow the directions for use.

Make sure your horse has access to clean water at all times. Scrub out buckets and troughs periodically and keep them filled.

Managing the nutritional needs of a horse confined in a stall or dry lot is fairly easy. Pasturing presents more challenges. If the pasture is large or lush or you are feeding many horses at once, it becomes difficult to control how much the horse is eating.

If he is pigging down much of the hay you intended for the herd, you may want to consider building a corral in which to feed him separately. He can be turned back out after he has eaten. If he is getting too fat on pasture grass alone, the corral will give you some place to put him on a diet for show season. The corral is also a handy place to keep the horse when the spring grasses come too lushly and quickly, threatening the horse with founder.

Your responsibility to his health and nutrition is year round. Don't toss him out in a pasture and forget about him once the show season is over. Horses deteriorate when their care is ignored. Unable to recover quickly from being neglected over the winter, they look and perform poorly when put back to work.

Pasturing can be wonderful for a horse. Just make sure you check him regularly. Don't assume that there is a lot of food out there just because the pasture looks green. The plants you see may be inedible weeds. Also don't assume he is getting enough to eat because hay is being fed. If he is in a herd of more dominant horses he may be getting very little. Keep in mind that shaggy winter hair can hide weight loss.

He is counting on you to take care of him. You don't want to wander out to the pasture in the spring to find your show horse has been starving.

Creating a Shiny Coat

Shiny coats come from four sources—good nutrition, grooming, exercise and prevention of sun damage.

All healthy horses shine. It is a reflection of the quality of their care. Feed your horse properly as has been discussed and he will shine, too. Some owners also add a tablespoon or so of vegetable or corn oil to the grain to help the coat.

Frequent grooming, particularly brushing with a soft brush, will coax the coat to an even higher gloss. Many professional riders also apply coat conditioners or light oils occasionally. To apply an oil or conditioner, place some on your hands or a cloth and smooth it over the horse. A little goes a long way. You want to lightly coat the hair, but not use so much that the hair appears greasy. After you are done, go over the horse's body with a soft brush to work the conditioner or oil into the coat. The best time to treat the horse is when he is wet after a bath, but it works on dry hair as well. Some stables even give their horses hot oil treatments. Oils and conditioners keep the hair from becoming overly dry and promote shine and softness.

Exercise also makes the horse shinier. The shine is a sign of his internal fitness. That's why many of the show horses are so shiny. As they work they become more fit and the circulation increases to the skin and hair follicles. The follicles become healthier and the hair shinier.

When your horse gets sweaty from the exercise, rinse him off if temperatures permit. The horse will be more comfortable and the rinse will rid the hair of the salty sweat residue.

Keeping the shine isn't always easy. The greatest single external cause of dull hair is the sun. Sun can burn a horse's hair just as it can burn your skin. Sun-damaged hair has a red, fuzzy cast to it. While it still shines some, it is not as shiny has as hair that has not been damaged. One of the reasons that high-level show horses are so shiny is that most are kept in stalls. The sun only touches their coats occasionally.

To keep your horse's gloss, put a light sheet on him when he is out in the sun if it is practical to do so. The sheet offers good protection except in areas where it gets too hot to use them. It also helps keep the annoying flies off his body.

For a horse that spends only part of his time outdoors, you might consider turning him out in the early evening, rather than during the day.

During the show season blanket the horse during cool days or evenings. Even a horse in summer coat can get a little shaggy from cooler temperatures. He may grow longer hair or get a dense, fuzzy look to his coat. Horses that are blanketed tend to have coats that are shorter and sleeker.

Conditioning

A horse in top physical shape looks, feels and performs better than a flabby horse. He is less likely to sustain injuries and tends to work more happily because the effort has become easier for him.

Getting your horse in good shape and keeping him in shape throughout the show season is one of the best things you can do for him and for your dreams of success. He will be able to give you more and perform to a higher level.

If your horse is the active type, it will be fairly easy to get him in shape for the show season. This is especially true if he spends lots of time out playing in the pasture. He'll be partially in shape just from play. More difficult to condition is the horse that is not very active on his own or one that is confined to a stall. Since he does little without your being there to exercise him, you will have to work longer and harder to get him fit.

If you are practicing or trail riding a great deal with the horse, he may be in shape already. But if practice sessions are low key or the horse remains flabby, you may want to make a more concerted effort to increase his fitness.

Start at twenty minutes to a half hour of good, solid work five to six days a week. This could be under saddle, on a lunge line, long-lining or any combination of these activities.

The ground work might seem a bit pointless with a horse that is broke to ride, but it can be quite useful. It adds variety, and the exercise unmounted allows you to work the horse at gaits you might not have wanted to under saddle. For example, one of the best conditioning gaits is a brisk trot, but if you are riding western your practice sessions will not include a brisk trot.

Also, if for any reason you need to keep riding sessions short, you can still get the horse in shape by adding lunging to the routine.

The ground work also allows you to watch the horse as he works, a luxury you do not have while mounted.

When conditioning the horse, let him walk when he needs to catch his breath, then put him back to work. As he finds the work increasingly easy, boost the time to forty-five minutes, then an hour, alternating faster gaits with slower ones. If he seems to be getting extremely tired at any time, walk him until he is cool, then put him away. You've pushed too hard and need to lighten the work. Pushing him when he is overly tired can cause injuries.

Just how fit the horse needs to be depends on what you will use him for. A horse that can work at a good pace for around an hour with a few rests in between is adequately fit for most types of showing. Some horses may need to be much more fit, depending on the class.

The horse does not, however, need to work the full time every day. You can alternate shorter workouts with a few longer ones in the week and he will be in nice shape for your show. A fit, well-cared-for horse also will live longer and continue to appear young and strong long into his elder years.

A fit horse has a particular look, more streamlined and less chunky. To the touch his muscles will be quite firm, and he will lose much of the squishy fat that dominated much of his body during his idle days. He will not look quite the same as a horse that is at his appropriate weight but not in shape. Look at the horses at the shows you attend and notice those that are truly fit. The fit horse looks the part of the athlete—lean, strong and able. Even his barrel will look less rounded, not protruding much to the sides or at the underline.

Shoeing

Your horse's hoof length and type of shoe are essential to his soundness and performance. Proper shoeing is important all season long, but especially during show season. Your horse cannot do his best if his shoeing is way past due or has been done improperly.

To help his performance, your horse should be shod specifically for the type of work he is doing. Just any shoes won't do. There are many different kinds of shoes with many different purposes. Just as you would need different

shoes for jogging and hiking, a horse competing in Western Pleasure needs
to be shod differently from one competing in Stock Horse or English Pleasure.
The owner of the western horse wants shoeing that will encourage smooth,
fluid motion. The owner of the stock horse wants shoeing that will help the
horse do quick turns and sliding stops. The owner of the saddleseat-style
English horse wants shoeing that will enhance high motion.

The farrier tailor makes shoes and trims the hoof specially for these classes
and your horse.

This is not the same thing as corrective shoeing. Corrective shoeing is
trimming the hoof and perhaps building the shoe to help the horse stand and
move straighter. Unless you are showing the horse in halter or his motion is
so erratic he is hitting himself with his hoofs, you probably do not need
corrective shoeing. It's a matter of choice. Some people have it done as a
matter of aesthetics.

Whether you choose corrective shoeing or not, it still is important to have
the horse shod specially for the classes in which he is showing.

Select a farrier who is experienced in shoeing horses that compete in your
classes. Ask other owners who they use. If your current farrier is just nailing
the same kind of shoes on all the horses, he or she many not have the
background it takes to shoe your horse properly for the show ring.

When the farrier comes, talk to him or her about what you are doing with
the horse, and ask for recommendations about the type of shoe and length
of hoof. If your horse is competing in a range of very different classes, such
as English and western, choose a more general shoe, or the shoe for the
horse's best class.

As the farrier works, have him or her explain what is being done and how
it will impact the horse's way of going. It will help you better understand
the mechanics of shoeing and hoof length.

Grooming

A well-groomed horse is appealing to the judge's eye and tells him or her
that you are competent, take good care of your horse and take showing
seriously. A badly groomed horse does just the opposite. It says you either
don't know how or don't care, both of which are disastrous impressions.

A judge for smaller shows once told me of his constant amazement at how little effort some exhibitors put into grooming their horses. They take all the time to prepare for and attend the show, then fail to do the little things that could help them succeed. He has seen horses come in the ring dirty, shaggy and with their hair still curled with many-days-old sweat. Some are obviously poorly cared for, are too thin or have bare hoofs that are chipped and broken. Some horses are so fat they struggle through their classes.

Judges notice all of these things, and it detracts from the performances. They also notice when horses are fit, well cared for and well groomed. Good care and grooming offers you the chance to make a good impression with the judge.

It is not enough to just give the horse a bath and trim the whiskers from his nose. That is merely the beginning. Many high-level riders spend an hour grooming one horse for the show ring.

Grooming does for the horse what makeup does for a movie star. Grooming is not that hard to learn. It just takes some time, practice and the desire to make your horse look really sharp.

The techniques you use must be for your specific breed of horse. Grooming is similar for every breed, but not exactly the same. Grooming an Arabian is different from grooming an Appaloosa or a Saddlebred. One of the cosmetic touches that can be applied to the Saddlebred, false hair pieces, would even be illegal in the ring on most other breeds.

When you groom the horse, you are helping him conform to a certain expectation of appearance for that breed. Although it is up to you whether to conform to that or not, you are less likely to do well if you choose not to. Your competitors are grooming their horses that way for a reason—they believe it helps them succeed. Unless you believe some aspect would be harmful to your horse or is offensive to you, follow the commonly used grooming techniques for your breed.

The best way to learn is hands-on. If you know someone showing at a high level, ask him or her to teach you. At horse shows you could also go to one of the farms stabled there, find the head groom and ask if you can watch him or her for a while. Approach the groom when the activity level is fairly low. You are more likely to get a good response than if you try when the groom is in a mad rush to get a number of horses ready.

When you watch the groom work, note the grooming supplies and how they are used. Ask questions. For a really hard-core course in grooming, offer your time to a stable as assistant groom for horse shows.

In general a well-groomed horse of nearly any breed looks sleek, shiny and clean. The body hair and hair of the mane and tail do not stick out or look fuzzy. All of the clipped areas—usually the nose, bridle path, ears, legs and long bristly hairs around the eyes—are cropped close. They are freshly clipped for each show. The whiskers are clipped every day. Hoofs usually are sanded until they feel smooth as glass, then one or more polishes are applied. The polishes match the hoof color or are clear.

Light oils or dressings are applied around the nose and eyes. Body dressings are lightly smoothed or sprayed on the coat. The crest of the mane and dock of the tail are coated with oil, a hair gel or petroleum jelly to keep stray hairs down.

You might find it helpful to get a book on grooming from your library or bookstore. There are a number on the market. Make sure if you use a book that it is fairly current and addresses showing at your level. Some books address only very basic grooming. You need more than that. Also read your show rule book for rules that apply to grooming.

Final Preparations

It's helpful if you can get someone to assist you in the last few moments immediately before you go in the ring. To this person falls the duty of the last-minute grooming. The assistant, bearing a cloth, hair brush and body brush, will wait for you by the gate.

After you have warmed up the horse for the ring, the assistant will quickly clean up the horse while you are waiting for the gate to open. The mane and tail should be brushed. If the tail drags the ground, it should be kept up in a ribbon until the hair is brushed out immediately before you enter the ring. The ribbon keeps the tail from dragging in the dirt and being stepped on. Just make sure you remember to have the ribbon removed before you go in.

Your assistant should also smooth any body hair that has gotten roughed and wipe mud and debris from the horse's body, hoofs and tack. This includes wiping the saliva from the bit and body. Some horses splatter white, foamy saliva down their chests and legs. It's all right if the horse gets saliva on himself in the class, but you want to enter the ring clean. Salivating like this is normal. (If your horse seems to be salivating more than normal, have a veterinarian examine him.)

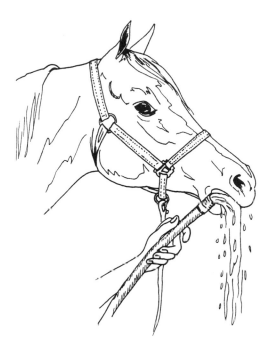

To rinse food debris from the horse's mouth prior to bridling, gently insert a hose into the corner of the mouth. Take care to make sure the water pressure is low and that you don't get water in the nostrils.

Don't let your horse eat anything immediately before you ride him. Green foods turn his saliva green, which looks horrible. Carrots produce an even worse effect. They can make the saliva rust colored, making it appear the horse's mouth is bleeding. If your horse has had a snack, before bridling him you can rinse his mouth out with a syringe full of water. A garden hose also works fine. Just turn it on low and gently slide it a few inches into the corner of his mouth (see illustration above). It only takes a moment to rinse his mouth of all the debris. It will keep the horse from foaming colors in the ring and give your assistant an easier time cleaning him up just prior to the class.

Your assistant's final duty is a quick check of your appearance. He or she will make sure your number is straight, boots are clean, tie is straight, and no hairpins are sticking out. It also is a good idea to check the tightness of the cinch, make sure the bit is straight in the horse's mouth, the tack is on correctly, and that the saddle pad has not slid off to the side.

This final preparation will help you and the horse look extra sharp in the ring.

If you don't have an assistant, you can do the last-minute check yourself. When you go over to the warmup ring, take a small bucket containing a hand-held mirror, cloth and hair and body brushes. Set the bucket nearby, out of the way of the horse traffic. A little before you go in the ring, hop off the horse and give him a quick grooming check, brush his mane and tail and check the tack. Use the mirror to check your own appearance. Take care not to get dirty during these preparations. Roll up the bottom of your pants or chaps to keep them from dragging in the dirt while you are on the ground, then roll them back down when you get on the horse.

Appearances at Home

Grooming doesn't stop when the show is over. It is not necessary for the horse to be show groomed at home but do stick to some minimum standards. Don't let your horse go to seed between shows.

After the show, wipe off the petroleum jelly, dressings and oils you applied to him. Strip the hoof polish off with rubbing alcohol, then put on a hoof conditioner. The sanding and polishes are hard on the hoofs and contribute to dryness and brittleness. You need to replace moisture and protect the hoofs.

At home brush your horse frequently to promote coat health. Keep him clipped and looking nice. Be particularly diligent about clipping the bridle path. Few things make a horse look worse than a bridle path with a few months' growth. Also keep his mane and tail free of major tangles. It will save you time later. It is easier to keep up on the tangles than spend an afternoon trying to comb out a tail that has become a solid, entangled mass.

Your horse's appearance affects your impression of him. It is human nature. The better he looks, the better you will feel about his ability to compete. Mentally you are constantly comparing your horse to others you see at shows and stables. But you usually see them at their best, sleek and groomed. You see yours in his everyday shagginess. You may love him, but you still will view his talents more positively if he looks good. Your positive view of him will increase your confidence in the ring. Remember that all horses, even those sleek, stunning ones you see in the ring, have their ugly days.

It takes little work or time to help your horse look better at home. The grooming sessions are also pleasant for the horse and give the two of you time to get to know each other better.

WHAT YOU CAN DO RIGHT AWAY TO IMPROVE

- Review the tack and clothing you are using in the ring now. Make sure it is in good shape, of current style and fits.
- Have your hat blocked.
- Begin a conditioning program for your horse.
- Review your feeding practices to determine if you are meeting the horse's needs as well as you could be.
- Find a top-notch farrier for your horse.
- Take steps to preserve the shine of the horse's coat as has been discussed.

WHAT YOU CAN DO IN THE FUTURE

- Start planning for the new outfit you want by observing what your competitors are wearing and by talking with the salespeople who specialize in rider wear.
- Begin replacing outdated and worn out show tack. It's easier on the budget if you do this gradually. Replacing tack may not be as expensive as you think, since often tack stores will allow you to trade in your old tack if it is in good shape. This can cut your bill for the new tack. You also may be able to buy used tack in good condition.
- Launder and press your clothes, shine your boots and clean your tack before every show.
- Learn grooming techniques from an experienced groom, and make sure your horse looks his best at every show.
- Take a moment before every class for last-minute grooming.

Selecting Classes

At small shows, everyone shows in nearly every class. In one weekend, a rider might compete in more than a dozen classes with the same horse. It's fun, and good experience for a well-rounded rider.

But at the larger shows, this kind of approach is not only impractical, but unsuccessful. Large shows often have more than a hundred classes. Competition is stiff, and the horses are more specialized in what they do. Like people, horses tend to have some things they do particularly well and some things they don't. The horses competing at high levels are entered only in those classes that are their very best. That is done to allow training to be more focused and specialized, to develop the horse's skills and physical strength for what he does best. It increases the horse's excellence in those classes so he places higher in them.

At the shows you attend, the number and type of classes you enter should be determined by your skills, your horse's skills, the size of show and what your competitors are doing. Your strategies and class selections change as you go to increasingly larger shows.

. . . .

SMALL SHOWS

If you are regularly showing in the smaller shows where competitors take the same horses in nearly every class, you can do the same thing and be competitive. Sampling a lot of classes is good experience and you'll enjoy the variety. But do keep in mind that if there is an unusually large number of classes or the judge is working you harder than usual, going in all the classes may be too much for your horse.

Six classes a day is a lot for a horse, even at a small show. I would not enter a horse in more than that. Fewer is better. It isn't a question of if the horse can do it. It is whether he should. I know one person who took her horse in twenty classes in one weekend. That's ten classes a day—way too many for most horses. At that number, toward the end of the show the horse literally starts dragging his hoofs along the ground in the ring.

How many classes is a sensible number for your horse depends on him. Listen to what he tells you. If at the end of a show he seems extremely tired, that was probably too many classes for him. Next time enter him in fewer. If toward the end of the show he still seems alert and ready to work, he is handling the classes well and might be able to do more, within reason.

Some horses worked to exhaustion at every show eventually start trying to slide through performances with minimal effort even in their early classes. They learn to save their energy. Trainers sometimes apply the same psychology when teaching an overly fast horse to canter slowly. The trainer asks the horse to canter, then lets him go as fast as he wants. Around and around they go until eventually the horse gets tired and tries to slow to a walk— but then the trainer makes him continue cantering. The horse, tired from his earlier speed, finds this unpleasant. Before too long, when asked to canter the horse will go slow from the start. He is saving his energy in the belief that he may have to canter a long time.

The horse that goes into too many classes every time he is shown may adopt the same strategy. He may try to pace himself, and that makes it harder on you as the rider to get a good performance from him. You still can get it by pushing him harder, but it will be more difficult to get the best effort from him.

Showing repeatedly in a large number of classes also may sour him on the show ring. Any enjoyment and interest he may have had for the work fades. Sometimes this just makes the horse bored with the work. In more extreme cases, however, it can make him cranky and resentful of ring work. Riding a horse that hates showing can be a chore.

The most enjoyable horses to show are those willing to give the performance their best effort every time the gate opens. They do so because the rider demands it and they are not repeatedly worked to exhaustion. The desire to please is also part of most good show horses.

Help your horse be a good show horse by not overshowing him. Enjoy the little shows, go in lots of classes, but don't go in so many in one day that you ride the horse into the ground. Keep the number of classes sensible.

Go for quality, not quantity. When you need to eliminate a few classes from your schedule at a show, get rid of the ones that you enjoy the least, or the ones in which your horse usually places the lowest.

In selecting specific classes, you can go in almost anything that appeals to you within the limits of your skills, the horse's ability and tack required. I would suggest sampling a lot of different kind of classes. When you decide on which you enjoy the most or have the greatest aptitude for—they're usually one and the same—concentrate your practice and showing on them, but take occasional forays into other classes and areas. My specialty is the saddleseat form of English Pleasure, but that is not the sole point of my interest. I've ridden hunt seat, western, Stock Horse, Western Riding, sidesaddle, Trail, most forms of equitation and gymkhana. Some of these I like very much, and may delve into again in the future.

If you haven't been showing horses long, you many want to concentrate your efforts on just a couple of classes at first instead of trying to take on everything at once. Pick one riding style, like western or English, then ride in the classes for that one style. When you become more confident and are happy with your progress, try another style of riding. Most new riders start out riding western or hunter.

Every class you ride gives you a broader range of experience and skill. You will find as you gain more experience that the basic principles behind most forms of riding are the same. What you learn in one area will help you more deeply understand another. What I learned on my stock horse improved my English riding. What I learned in English improved my western, and so on. To the rider, most classes interrelate.

LARGER SHOWS

The larger the show, the fewer classes your horse can be competitive in. That sounds a bit strange since larger shows have even more classes than the little ones, but it is true. The larger the show is, the greater degree of specialization of the horses in the classes. That makes them tough competitors.

To go against them, you will combine your best abilities with those of the horse. You can determine what those abilities are by asking yourself: What are my best classes? What are the horse's best classes? What are our best classes as a team?

First, let's deal with the horse. To be competitive at a high level, your horse must become a specialist. The ability is already inside him. To develop it, you will concentrate his training and his showing in the classes in which he has the greatest aptitude. You won't enter the other classes with him. He is capable of doing other classes, but his true aptitude is in one area. His effort would best be directed to that area, rather than in classes where his performance will be mediocre.

Remember that at this level of showing, the classes in which he is mediocre will be populated with horses that excel at those classes. Your are matching his average skill against their exceptional skill. He is at a disadvantage and will not be able to compete successfully against them.

He will be most successful in the classes at which he excels. And that is where you want to concentrate most of your work.

There is another reason as well to enter the horse only in the classes in which he excels. It saves his best effort for the classes where that effort is most likely to win a high placing. The horse's energy is limited.

When you take him in a class that is not one of his better ones, you are taking away from the effort he could have given in the classes in which he was most able to succeed. In other words, you perhaps are trading in a few high placings for lots of much lower placings.

When he goes in a limited number of classes, he is more likely to look brighter, happier, wear his ears forward and not look bored. His movements will be less sluggish and heavy, and more fluid and energetic. You may or may not feel these differences in him, but they are visible to the judge. At the larger shows these things really matter. It is those kinds of seemingly minor points that can make the difference between placing high and placing low.

As the shows get bigger, the differences between the horses that are winning and those that are placing lower get smaller and more subtle. At a national or world-level show, even the horses that don't place may be exceptional.

Big errors that could drop a horse out of competition become increasingly rare at these shows. In the absence of errors and with the whole class full of good horses, it is the seemingly small points that make the difference between winning and losing. These points can include the expression on the horse's face, smoothness of transitions and physical beauty. Classes also can be won or lost based on if he wears his ears up or back, looks labored or energetic, moves fluidly or stiffly, holds his tail up or clamped down. The judges also look at the suitability of the rider to the horse, if the overall picture presented is pleasing or awkward and if the rider seems to be struggling or relaxed.

This is the big league. Here, you start seeing a different kind of horse. At the small, all-breed shows, many of the horses were bred for basic versatility and to produce good, sound, athletic horses. Their ability to do so many classes adequately is a tribute to their breeders. Some are bred for specific uses, but many are bred just to be good horses.

That rule doesn't hold true for many of the horses you see at the large shows. At these shows you begin seeing horses that have been bred for generations specifically for the development of a certain skill, then trained solely in that skill. You will see the saddleseat type of English horses that have been bred for high trot and upright bearings, western horses bred specifically for beauty and fluid motion and hunters bred for the hunter style. Some may be the offspring literally of generations of horses that excelled in one area. Occasionally you may even see the offspring of a national or world champion that was bred to another national or world champion. Although all of the horses at the show may be of the same breed, they are so vastly different in their purposes that they seem almost like different breeds.

This is the environment into which you step when you start showing at increasingly larger shows. You will succeed there by taking advantage of every edge that you can gain, and by cultivating a confidence in yourself and your horse. When you first begin attending larger shows, it can be quite intimidating. Don't underestimate yourself or your horse. Remember that you can be competitive as well. You have earned your place at this level. You have excelled at a lower level and now are ready to advance. Your horse is ready to advance, too. He has won over the competition at smaller shows, and he's up to the challenge of stiffer competition. You may not know it, but your competition may be as worried about you as you are about them.

You can be competitive at this level by concentrating your greatest effort on the classes you and the horse do best. You may be surprised at how far this can take you. A horse I had in my late teens went from being a little-show horse to winning national titles in the United States and Canada. The difference was specialization. The horse was given the opportunity and training to concentrate on what he could do best. By dropping the other classes and just concentrating on his potential skill, he had more room to develop that skill and became an exceptional competitor in that field.

When you start being more selective about what classes the horse should perform, you are doing two things—giving him the opportunity to develop a specialty, and saving his energy for his best classes. Each class he goes in uses up some of his energy. He gets more and more tired as the show progresses. His fatigue is mental as well as physical. In the classes he has to pay attention, follow directions, be in close proximity to strange horses and deal with the hubbub of the show around him. It causes stress. That and the physical demands of showing exhaust him.

Most successful riders limit the number of classes the horse enters according to how big the show is. The bigger the show is, the fewer classes the horse will be entered in. That allows the horse to put forth his best effort in the classes.

At mid-level shows, three or four classes a day is probably an average number a horse might be entered in. At high-level shows, two classes a day is more common. At a national or world level, most horses go in just one. One rider may bring many horses, each horse for a different class.

When trying to decide how many classes to take the horse in, also consider the horse's physical condition, the intensity of the class and the horse's age. A flabby horse may be tired after just one class and turn in lackluster performances in all the classes after that. It is important for the horse to be fit. He will be able to give you a greater effort in the classes and have better endurance.

Some classes also require a supreme physical effort. Examples are high-level English, Park Horse, Stock Horse and Western Equitation, which requires an extensive pattern. While a few horses can handle two of these in a day, for most horses one is plenty, regardless of the show size. A few classes a day are also plenty for most young horses. Young horses can't do as much as mature horses. When you push them too hard and make them go in too many classes, you risk injuries and mental burnout in the horse. Keep the workload at the show light. If it is a demanding class, just go in one a day. Two or perhaps even three are all right if the work is light and the show is short.

At first it may seem difficult to decide how to go about limiting the horse's classes. Faced with a premium book listing more than a hundred classes to choose from, it may seem a daunting chore. But regardless of the number of classes, it still comes down to the three questions: What are you good at? What is the horse good at? What are you good at together?

The horse is going to help you make the decision. He already has been telling you what he does best through his placings at other shows, his physical attributes and attitude. Listen to him. If he's been placing high in western and has the attributes of a good western horse, he should be entered in Western Pleasure.

You may like another class better, but his full potential can only be reached in the class for which he has a true aptitude. Trying to force him to be something he is not wastes his potential.

After the choice is made, you can help him develop his skill to its utmost potential by focusing his training specifically on that one area. Let's say the horse's aptitude is Western Pleasure. To develop that, you will shift training practices and conditioning to focus specifically on western. You will drop other things you were doing with him that would conflict with his new goal. For example, you may stop barrel racing with him. It doesn't hurt him to do both, but to bring him to the level of refinement of the western skill that you now want, you need to work him in tasks that develop western skill.

That doesn't mean that the horse has to do the same thing day after day for the rest of his life. You can still try new things with him, take him for pleasure rides and give him variety in his workouts, as was discussed in Chapter 3. But your primary work should be on the skills it takes for the classes in which he is most suited. Horses, like people, prefer doing the things they do well. You are not doing the horse a disservice by concentrating on those skills.

If you want to take him in more than one class, choose classes that require similar skills, like English and Driving, Western Pleasure and Western Equitation, Stock Horse and Western Riding, and so on. Avoid mixing classes that require greatly different skills, like Stock Horse and English Pleasure.

The horse plays the leading role in determining the classes you will ride because he has a limited number of things he can do well. There may be a lot of things he can do, but only a few will be at a competitive level at big shows. The horse is destined by his build and temperament to be good at certain things. The rider has the same concerns, but is not as limited, since most styles of riding have the same basic elements. You as the rider have more flexibility in doing well in a class than the horse does.

But your aptitudes do contribute to class selection. Like the horse, you are better at some classes than others. By concentrating practice on your best classes, you will excel in them to an even greater extent. You will become, in your own way, a specialist in certain classes, although you may participate in a wide variety.

The best possible situation in the show ring is to match a rider who excels in a class, with a horse that excels in the same class. That is the most successful combination possible. When you are shopping for a new horse, that is your goal—to find a partner with skills that will complement your own. You want a horse with the best skills possible in that class.

With your current horse, you may or may not have that combination. If you don't, it is not necessarily a bad thing. His skill in a particular area may offer you the opportunity to learn more and do better in a new class. There is nothing wrong with riding a horse that is better at something than you are, as long as the class is one in which you are genuinely interested. He can teach you a lot, and help you place well in a class that you might not do well in otherwise.

The situation that you want to avoid is having a horse with which you have unreconcilable interests. The class that is his best is your worst or most disliked. Or, perhaps the class that is your best is impossible for him to perform. If this happens, the best thing for both of you is to sell the horse.

Many riders have a number of show horses, each for a specific class or classes. The rider takes each horse in his best classes, but you can be sure that among those horses is one that excels in the same classes that are the rider's best.

You probably already know what classes are your best. They are the ones in which you are placing well, enjoy and feel competent in. If there is a class you are not doing well in but still enjoy, that also might have the potential to become one of your best. It may be that your skill in that area just hasn't developed yet.

. . . .

HORSE SHOW CLASS SELECTION

When selecting classes at shows, pick those that best suit the skills of yourself and the horse. In pleasure classes, it is particularly important that the class matches his skills. In equitation, it is more important that the class matches your skills.

Let's say that you are going to ride Western Pleasure, and are faced with a premium book full of a hundred classes. Go through the class list and circle all western classes that you and the horse are eligible to enter, then start weeding them out. There may be a lot of them.

The best classes would depend on your circumstances, specifically: How old is the horse? How experienced is he? Is he/she a mare, stallion or gelding? How old are you? How experienced are you? Who is your competition? Are you an amateur or professional trainer? (Professionals earn money for training or giving lessons or clinics. Amateurs do not rely on horses for income.) All of these questions will have a bearing on your chances for success in each class.

With the answers to these questions in mind, look up the definitions of all the classes you are considering entering, then choose which would offer the best chance of success. In any large division such as English or western, there may be a lot of classes, such as Western Pleasure Limit, Western Pleasure Open, Western Pleasure Maiden, and so on. Here are some of the common classes often offered at mid-size to large shows:

MAIDEN.   For horses that have not yet won a first-place ribbon, this is a good class for young or inexperienced horses. Your horse, if he qualifies for this class, would be pitted against horses just like himself, giving him a greater chance of success than against veteran horses.

NOVICE.   For horses that have not yet won three first-place ribbons, this class will have horses a little more experienced than in the maiden class, but not by much. It's an excellent class for the young and inexperienced.

LIMIT.   For horses that have not yet won six first-place ribbons, this is another good class for a horse that is young or inexperienced.

JUNIOR HORSE.   Specifically for horses under four, this is the perfect class for the young horse. Again, he will be pitted against horses just like himself, and won't have to go up against mature horses.

LADIES TO RIDE.   Just for women and girls, the value of this class depends on who your competition is. If your primary competition has been from a male rider, you can screen him out by going in this class.

GENTLEMEN TO RIDE.   This is the same class as the one above, only for men and boys. If you are male and your greatest competition is coming from female riders, you can screen them out by going in this class.

AMATEUR TO RIDE.   There are many different amateur classes. Usually you will see an Amateur to Ride for adults and a number of sections for young riders. There may also be classes that require that the amateur also be the owner. All of these are good classes for amateurs to enter. Although these classes are judged on the horse, the quality of the horse's performance depends greatly on the rider. Amateur classes recognize this.

In entering this class, you will be competing against riders who are not professionals. Professionals tend to have an edge in classes because they can get a higher level of performance from horses. It's their business to know how. The amateur classes are the only ones that screen out trainers. All the others are open to them. But that doesn't mean amateur classes are easy pickings. Being an amateur and being amateurish are two very different things. Many amateurs are extremely accomplished riders.

OPEN.   When you enter this class, you are potentially pitting your horse against every horse of his type on the grounds. Anyone can enter this class. Open classes at small to mid-size shows aren't much different from any other class at the show, but at the big shows there is a world of difference. At large shows, the open class usually offers the toughest competition. It is usually populated with trainers riding the highest-caliber horses on the grounds.

CLASSES FOR SPECIFIC SEXES   —such as just for geldings, stallions or mares. These classes are a lot like the ladies- or gentlemen-to-ride classes. Their worth depends on your competition. For example, if you are riding a gelding and your greatest competition is from a mare, you can screen her out by entering a class just for geldings.

EQUITATION.   These are the only classes judged on the rider. All other classes are judged on the horse. (In the western division, you may see the equitation class named Western Equitation or Horsemanship. They are the same class.)

When picking classes, try to challenge yourself and the horse, but also keep an eye toward what would offer the best chance for success. Throw out any class that for some reason would be too easy a win, throw out those that offer little hope of success and make your best choices from what is left. A class that would be too easy, for example, would be if you were riding a horse that has only been shown a few times, but had won a regional championship in Western Pleasure. It would be unfair to take such a horse in a Western Pleasure Limit. Even though he is qualified, he has far surpassed that level of class.

When riding a youngster that hasn't much experience, whether you are a professional or amateur, your best chances for success would be in maiden, limit, novice, or junior horse, whichever apply. There are professional trainers in the classes, but the horses are at similar levels. Your worst choices for him would be open. It would pit him against the best horses on the grounds, which is probably more than he can handle right now.

If you are a trainer riding an experienced horse, your best class would be open. Although it is the most difficult, it is also the one that will make your reputation. Open is the testing ground where reputations are made. Success there proves the quality of your abilities as a trainer. Other classes for you would be the classes based on the sex of the horse or rider. If you are a trainer riding an inexperienced horse, go in the classes specifically for such horses.

If you are an amateur showing an experienced horse, your best bets are to stick to the amateur classes. They are made for you. If you are showing a superstar kind of horse, you might want to go in open, too, to give the trainers a run for the money. Otherwise avoid open, since it represents your least chance for success.

When showing at a high level, you also may encounter a few judges who are prejudiced against a horse going in both amateur and open classes. You may run into this whether you are riding the horse in both classes, or you are riding in the amateur class and having a professional ride your horse open. The problem can crop up either way. Some judges just don't think a horse should do both. They see it not just as two types of classes, but different types of horse—an open-level horse and an amateur-level horse.

Most judges do not share this antiquated opinion. They believe an amateur should be able to ride any horse that he or she can handle well. They do not try to deny the amateurs the right to ride the best horses. But be aware that occasionally you may encounter a judge who doesn't think open-quality horses should appear in amateur classes.

WHAT YOU CAN DO RIGHT AWAY TO IMPROVE

- Assess your horse's abilities to determine what he does best.
- Assess your own abilities to determine what you do best.
- Make a list of the shows you want to attend this year.

WHAT YOU CAN DO IN THE FUTURE

- Increasingly focus training and practice to develop the best skills in the horse and yourself.
- Cultivate an awareness of your horse's endurance levels and how his performance changes from class to class.
- When you receive premium books for shows, select with care the classes you want to enter. Keep in mind the chances for success in each and who the competition might be.
- Avoid entering classes that fall close to one another. The horse will do better if there is enough space in between classes that he can rest.

Preparation for Show Success

Fun and success at a show rely almost as much as what goes on outside the ring as what happens inside of it. Good preparations can help you gain an edge over competitors, make the show a lot more enjoyable and reduce stress on yourself and the horse.

Ever arrived at a show and realize you left something important at home, like the bridle? Had to rush into a class because you didn't have enough time to get ready for it? Seen your horse get so cranky at a show that he behaved badly in his classes? Gotten so tired that you moved through your classes like a zombie? These kinds of things are common, but they also lessen your chances of doing well and enjoying the show. Good preparations are a matter of doing everything you can to see that when you go into the class, you and the horse are ready and able to do your best.

HOME PREPARATIONS

Nothing adds to show anxiety like arriving late, rushing to prepare for a class or forgetting to take something you need. We all do it at one time or another. You can cut down on these kinds of errors by taking a little extra time at home with the packing and other pre-show preparations. It can mean the difference between having a nice, enjoyable show and spending most of your time dashing around in a panic.

Cleaning Up

Before you pack a single thing, make sure it is clean. Showing in dirty tack or clothes is a poor reflection on your horsemanship. Before every show, clean your tack and wash grooming towels, brushes, leg wraps and the horse cooler, blanket or sheet, whichever you are using. Wash or dry-clean your show clothes.

Putting dirty things on a clean horse defeats the purpose of cleaning the horse. Everything must be clean. If your tack contains silver, it should be polished frequently. You have the silver because it looks nice. It won't look nice if it is tarnished. It is better to use tack with no silver than to ride with tarnished silver.

Packing

Packing for a horse show is more challenging than packing for an extended European vacation. It is easy to forget something you need. It may be some minor thing like a brush, or it could be the saddle pad.

You can avoid the trauma of forgotten things by making a list of every single thing you need at the show, from the hay to the hoof pick. Include all of your clothing, all the tack and even the big things you think you'll never forget, like the saddle. Keep it orderly, listing all similar things together under headings such as "tack," "feed," "stall-cleaning equipment," "grooming equipment," "washing gear," "miscellaneous horse items," "clothes and boots," "makeup and hair," "miscellaneous people items," and so on. Then make at least three copies of that list. You can use it to pack for every show, year after year, updating it as needed.

The list is particularly nice the first few shows of the season after time off has made you a little rusty with your packing.

Tape one of the master lists inside the horse trailer's tack-room door, and leave it there. Tape another somewhere in the house. Then take the third copy and cut it into mini lists. Paste the list of grooming and washing supplies to the inside lid of the box of grooming supplies, put the feed list in the room where you keep the feed and so on. It is repetitious, but it can help make sure you don't leave behind anything you need.

Even if you rely on a trainer to provide a majority of the supplies and equipment needed at a show, make a list of the things you are responsible for bringing, such as your clothes.

I keep a list of everything I need permanently affixed on the inside of a closet door. When I'm packing, I open the door, read the list and pile in front of the closet everything that must go to the show. Then I check through everything to make sure it is all there, and pack it out to the vehicle. During the middle of the show season I could pack in my sleep, but I still use the list to double-check what I'm doing.

The most serious memory lapse I've had was when I left behind my English jodhpur boots. Of course I didn't realize it until I was at the show, a six-hour drive away from where my boots were sitting in the closet. There were a lot of English boots at the show, but they were on other people's feet. And most of those people were in my class. This was a regional championship show and I needed to be concentrating on the upcoming competition, but instead I spent my time running around the show grounds looking for someone with jodhpur boots my size. The best I could borrow was a pair two sizes too small. I rode my regional class feeling like my toes were in vise grips.

Lists can help save you from such unnecessary problems, and it is also helpful to have just one person do the packing. That avoids the "but I thought you packed it!" problem. Pack everything yourself and you will know what you have. If you do need assistance, assign your helpers to specific areas, like packing all of the supplies on the grooming list, or all of the things on the tack list.

The final point is to make sure all the things you pack are usable. For example, if you are going to wear a new outfit at the show, try all of it on first at home to make sure it fits and matches.

Precautions

Minor accidents happen. You can break tack, split seams, pop buttons and spill bottles of hoof black on your show clothes. It's wise when packing to add a few items for crisis relief to make sure these little mishaps don't keep you from entering your classes.

Pack a complete second set of show clothes if you have one. Also include a small sewing kit, safety pins, black electrical tape, scissors, pliers, a screwdriver, hammer and anything else you believe might come in handy. These items can be used to make many small repairs of tack, clothing and equipment. The tape, for example, is good for everything from holding down a flopping strap to plugging a leak in a hose.

Early Grooming

Unless the show offers better facilities than you have at home, it is usually easier to do most of the clipping of the horse at home. There are fewer distractions there and you are not under a time crunch. The last thing you want is to have to rush through clipping or skip it entirely because the show schedule has been altered and you have run out of time.

Clipping the horse at home will simplify and reduce the time you need to spend grooming the horse before the class. You will still need to trim the horse's whiskers again before your class, but the bridle path, ears, face and legs should be fine for the duration of most shows.

Whether or not you should bathe the horse before you go is a matter of individual preference. Go ahead if you have a good place to do it and are showing that day. His cleanliness won't last much longer. If you have to show early in the morning, it is better to get up extremely early and give the bath then, weather permitting. When you give a bath the day before, the horse has only a partial chance of being clean by class time. A sheet on the horse and lots of clean bedding in the stall will help but will not guarantee he'll be clean the next day. Some horses are quite fastidious, but others seem to like being grubby and may defeat your best efforts to keep them clean.

Pasture horses present an additional challenge. A horse given a bath then turned out in the pasture has a slim chance of being clean the next day. You may want to just save the bath for the show grounds. If you confine the pasture horse overnight so he stays clean, consider lunging him the next day at the show before your classes start. Some horses unused to stalls get wound up when confined.

Finally, keep in mind how the route to the show grounds might affect your horse's cleanliness. If you have to pass over a stretch of dirt or gravel during the hot weather, your horse is going to be coated with dust by the time you unload him. Save the bath for the show grounds.

Regardless of how you clean the horse for your first class, remember that he needs to be equally clean for all your classes. There's no rule that says a horse should only be washed once per show. Nothing looks more unprofessional than manure stains and grime on a show horse. Wash him as often as you need to have him clean, weather permitting. If he's light colored, that may be quite often. When I had a light gray horse with four knee-high white socks, I felt like I spent half my life in the show wash rack.

When the weather is a little cool, put a cooler on the horse and walk him dry after bathing. It will help keep him from getting chilled.

Wait until the horse is dry before you do any other grooming. The damp hair can thwart your efforts. For example, if you try to apply hoof black and accidentally touch the brush to the hair at the coronet band, the damp hair will pull the black up the leg hair like a wick. You'll have big, black blotches on the leg.

Shoeing

Before you go to a show, check the horse's shoes to make sure they are on solidly, the horse doesn't need to be reshod and the hoofs are below the legal limit. Different breeds have differing rules on how long the hoofs can be and how much the shoes can weigh. This usually isn't checked at unrated shows, but is at big shows. If you are going to a large show, be particularly mindful of this. It is within the authority of the show officials to measure your horse's hoofs and pull and weigh a shoe. If you are over the limit, you will be disqualified.

Safe Shipping

Your primary responsibility when going to a show is to make sure the horse gets there unharmed.

Lessen the chance of injuries in the trailer by putting shipping boots on all four legs of the horse. Shipping boots are knee-high nylon or leather wraps lined with thick fleece. You can also use polo wraps over thick sheet cotton. Either way, the wraps should cover the entire leg from the knee down to the ground. Don't put them on so high that the back of the hoof is exposed. The wraps are there to protect the legs from bumps and scrapes, and to keep the horse from cutting himself with his own hoofs should he start to scramble in the trailer.

Some people also put special shipping helmets on their horses to keep them from being hurt if they bump their heads in the trailer. The helmets are usually leather lined with thick fleece.

Before you load the horse, do one last check of the trailer, its lights and hitch to make sure everything is working. It is also a good idea to check the interior of the trailer for sharp edges or protrusions on which the horse could be cut.

Scoop out old hay and dirt in the manger and replace it with new hay. If you want him to have any other snacks, cut them into little pieces. That's a good idea when feeding him outside of the trailer, too. Things like small, whole apples can lodge in the throat.

Open or close the trailer vents according to how warm it is outside and try to make him as comfortable as possible. If it is cold, blanket him.

Tie him in the trailer with enough slack so he can move his head around some, but not so much that he can get in trouble. If he can reach his head down to his knees when he is tied, he's way too loose. How tight he should be tied depends on him, but in general the tie will probably be about the right length if he can reach nearly to his chest. If he pulls back, he is most likely telling you that you have tied him too short.

On the way to the show, drive carefully and wear your seat belt. You may want to stop a few times along the way to check on him. If you hear a commotion in the trailer, stop as soon as possible to see what is causing it.

. . . .
ON THE GROUNDS

At the show, your performance and that of the horse are impacted by a wide variety of factors, including schedules, sleep, nutrition, how you handle nervousness and how the horse is warmed up. You've likely noticed the effects of some of these already. You do not ride as well when you are tired and worried about a class. The horse does not perform as well when he is tired, or is rushed into a class without being worked first.

All of these things can make a difference in your performances and placings in the ring. This is one of the areas where you can give your competitors the edge over you, or gain an edge over your competitors. For example, perhaps there is a party on the show grounds that goes long into the wee hours of the morning. You have the first class in the morning, at 7:30 A.M. To bathe and groom the horse and yourself, you estimate you'll have to be up at 5:00 A.M. You have the choice of not going to the party, going for a while but getting home at a reasonable hour or staying until the party breaks up at 2:00 A.M.

You should go to the party if you want to. Socializing is part of the fun of the shows. But it would be unreasonable to expect that you could stay until 2:00 A.M. and still be in top shape the next day for your class. You would also run the risk of sleeping in too late and being ill prepared for the class. By choosing this route, you would be giving your competitors an edge over you because you would be preventing yourself from being the best you could be. However, if you chose to go home at a modest hour, it would be you who would gain the edge, because you would be rested, prepared and at your best.

Arrival

Give yourself ample time to prepare for classes by arriving at the grounds early. The farther away the show is, the earlier you should arrive. Hauling is physically and mentally taxing for the horse. He needs time to unwind, get acclimated to his surroundings and rest before the classes begin. You need the lead time as well to pick up your number and other show information from the office, organize yourself, groom the horse and dress for the classes.

If you just rush to the show, throw the saddle on and go in your class, the horse is more likely to be on his worst behavior than if you allowed some time between arrival and riding the first class.

When attending small shows near your home, arriving two hours early at the grounds probably is sufficient, depending on what you need to do before the show starts. If it's a show you have not attended before, it's nice to give yourself a little extra time as well to get the lay of the land.

When attending shows that are farther away, such as a five-hour drive, consider going the night before. That gives both you and the horse overnight to rest from the journey. For extremely important or distant shows, consider going earlier yet. It is fairly common for horses attending world or national shows to arrive a week or more in advance. This gives the horses the chance to rest from the long journey and to settle into a routine. If there is a significant altitude change that could hamper the horse's ability to perform, consult your veterinarian about how long it would take for the horse to adjust adequately to the change.

Care at the Show

At the grounds, stick to the same feeding schedule as the horse had at home—the same foods given at the same times.

Occasionally a class is going to conflict with the feeding schedule. When this happens, feed after the class. You don't want him to be digesting a big meal while you are trying to work him in a class. If you have one of those horses that work poorly around mealtime when their stomachs are empty, give him a small amount of hay as a snack an hour or two before the class.

You can give him the rest of his hay after the class is done. Remember that when the horse is hot, he should not eat or drink until he is completely cool.

It is important as well that the horse get his rest at the show. His performance will suffer if he's not sleeping well. You can help him in a number of ways. Give him a lot of undisturbed time to sleep. He will sleep some at night, and may also take naps during the day. Your classes or practice time may interfere with this somewhat, but make sure he has time to sleep.

Many stables at large shows put up curtains to screen the horses off from the constant hubbub beyond the stalls. The curtains have drawbacks, but do make it is easier for the horse to sleep and relax. The curtains also help protect him from passersby clucking and poking at him.

If you notice your horse does not seem to be getting enough sleep at the shows or is overly excited in his stall by all the hubbub, you may want to screen off his stall with curtains. You can even use sheets or blankets. You could put them up throughout the show or just at night, whenever you think he needs them most. A lot of things happen at horse shows, even in the middle of the night. He might just be staying up all night watching and listening to it. Regardless of what you use, don't wrap up the stall so much that the horse is standing in dark isolation all day. It's better if he can see out into the barn aisle at least part of the time.

Throughout the show, keep his stall clean and his water fresh. You are going to ask him for his best effort. It is only fair that you give him your best. If there are days during the show that he is not showing, take him out for walks, or lunge or ride him lightly.

Practice and Warmup

Do the bulk of your practicing at home. Some people at shows practice their horses so much before the classes that the horses are exhausted before they enter the gate. That's unnecessary. If your horse does not know his stuff by the time he gets to the show, riding him into the ground at the show is not going to make up for it.

Practice is beneficial, as long as it is short. You should not be trying to teach the horse something new or trying to get him to do something at which he has consistently failed before. Those kind of sessions are for home. At the show, you should instead work on fine tuning. This includes such things as getting a few last-minute tips from your instructor, working through nervousness, getting acquainted with the arena, looking for hazards such as dips or wet spots and refining the horse's performance by insisting on his best. Practice can also help you get a feel for the horse, then design your ring strategy to match. Horses have lazy days, energetic days, grumpy days and happy days. You have to adapt somewhat in order to get the best performance. For example, you are going to have to push him harder if he is feeling grumpy or lazy. But if you rode him the same way when he was feeling wildly energetic, you likely would cause a blowup.

Keep your at-show practices to just what is needed. If you don't feel the need to practice, don't practice. If you are on a veteran horse, you might not need any practices at a show.

Whether you practice or not, the horse will need a brief warmup, ten to fifteen minutes or so, depending on the class. If the weather is cold, give him a little more time to warm up than if temperatures are mild. If the weather is quite hot, shorten the warmup a little.

Warmups make the body limber and start the mind thinking about work. It's not a good idea to go into the class without this preparation. The horse cannot perform adequately if his body has not been warmed up. Just keep the warmup time limited so you don't wear him out.

The exception to that is the hot horse. Depending on the performance you want from him, he may need to have a little energy skimmed off before you go in. A common practice with such horses is to lunge them earlier in the day, then put them away. Just before class time they get the regular ten-minute warmup, then go in. The lunging earlier in the day takes the edge off without diminishing the brilliance in the ring.

If you want to save energy, such as for a horse that has a lot of classes in one day, give him just enough warmup to get his muscles limbered, and then go in. If you practice a lot in between classes, he won't have much effort left for the classes.

After the Class

After a sweaty class, walk the horse until he is cool and dry. In cold weather put a cooler on him between classes, especially if he is sweaty (see illustration, page 106). It will keep him from becoming chilled.

When you have a sufficient time in between classes, take the horse back to his stall. This is like a coffee break for him. He can drink a little water, urinate and relax for a while. If you do not have time to untack him, tie him in the stall and keep an eye on him. The stall time is a good mental respite for the horse and will help refresh him for coming classes. In addition, there are some horses that will not urinate while a rider is on them. If it is hot, the breaks are also important to allow the horse to drink enough water so he doesn't dehydrate.

Some riders like to sit on their horses in between classes and watch the other classes. It is better when time permits to take the horse back to his stall than to sit on him at the ring.

Dealing with Weather

Horse shows are notorious for wildly fluctuating weather, especially in the early spring. It can be hot, freezing cold, rainy or even snowy. It is important to protect the horse and yourself from the weather as best you can.

When the horse is wet from sweat or being bathed, put a cooler on him and walk him dry. This is particularly important in cold weather to keep him from becoming chilled.

When it's extremely hot, keep the horse out of the direct sun as much as possible between classes. Heat tends to make horses listless, so efforts to relieve the heat will help him work a little better for you.

If you are tying the horse to a trailer, park in the shade when possible. If he is stabled, you can cool off the stable area by wetting down the ground in the aisle and setting up big fans to keep the air moving. You also can help him cool off by sponging or hosing cool water in places where his veins run close to the skin, such as on his lower legs or on the inside of his flanks. After his classes rinse him off completely, then walk him dry.

Make sure as always that he has a lot of cool, fresh water to drink. You also need to drink a lot of fluids and avoid the direct sun as much as possible. Between classes seek out the shade and get something to drink. But be careful not to drink a great deal immediately before your class, or it could slosh around in your stomach and make you feel ill. If possible, wear lightweight show clothes in the ring. And wear sunscreen.

If you start feeling faint while in a class, stop and ask for a time out. It is safer than potentially falling from the horse. If you feel faint in the lineup, dismount and ask for assistance.

Both for your sake and that of the horse, practice early in the morning or late at night when it is cooler.

Cold weather brings a different set of challenges. If the horse is accustomed to the cold and still has his winter coat, he can deal with it adequately as long as you take some precautions. Make sure he is thoroughly warmed up before you go in the ring and don't let him stand around when he is warm. For example, if your class has been delayed and you have already warmed up the horse, keep him walking until he goes in. After the class put a cooler blanket on him and walk him until his temperature normalizes and the sweat dries. He can get chilled after a workout, especially if he is sweaty.

A horse that has been body clipped (all the winter hair clipped off) or has shed his winter coat will have more difficulty coping with the cold and will need more assistance from you. The horse should be blanketed, especially at night. In extreme cold, double blanket him and put a hood on him if you have one.

After you have groomed him for his class, throw a cooler on him and leave it on until you are ready to ride him.

Give him a little extra time to warm up and keep him moving. His body heat will keep him warm during the warmup and class, but once he stops moving he can get cold rapidly. After his class, walk him dry with the cooler on, then take him back to the stall and blanket him. The cooler is also handy for throwing over the horse and saddle in the rain. It's not waterproof, but will protect both from getting wet for a time.

Keep the horse out of the rain, snow and wind as much as possible.

If there is warm water on tap anywhere on the show grounds, periodically take the horse buckets of warm water. In cold weather, he is more likely to drink warm water than icy-cold water. But make sure the water you are taking him is warm, not hot.

For yourself, always pack a slicker, hat cover, waterproof shoes or boots, and lots of warm clothing to any show that has even the slimmest chance of turning rainy or cold. The slicker and waterproof boots are extremely important, because if you get wet, you will become even colder. I once became so desperate at a soggy show after forgetting my waterproof boots that I wrapped my feet in garbage-can liners from the motel. It didn't work very well. Remember your boots.

Also see if you can find some long underwear that would fit under your show clothes. If that is too bulky, try the Spandex-and-cotton-mix clothing commonly worn for aerobics. It's stretchy, skintight and adds a little warmth. When you are riding you will warm up, but it does help to have a little extra clothing.

Shows are rarely canceled because of weather, although classes sometimes are postponed. In all the shows I've been to, I can think of only a few canceled because of adverse conditions—and one of those was because a volcanic eruption buried the show grounds in ash. Usually the show must go on. Prepare yourself as best you can.

Protecting Your Partner

Do everything possible at the show and at home to protect your horse from injury and illness. Keep him in good physical condition, feed him well and stay current on his vaccination, worming and shoeing schedules.

If the conditions in the ring pose a risk to the horse, withdraw from the classes. Bad conditions might include poor footing that could cause a strain to a muscle, ligament or tendon. If the conditions on the grounds are so bad that being at the show poses a risk to the horse, leave the show entirely. This might include things such as inadequate stabling. The horse's welfare is in your hands, and that must come first. He is your partner. Don't sacrifice him for a riding title.

If he becomes injured, give him time to heal. Don't push him back into the ring. Sometimes it is hard to wait, especially when it seems vital that you ride the class. My family has had to withdraw horses from regional and even national competition because of injuries—after having traveled hundreds of miles and invested years in training to get the horse there. It's heart breaking.

Some people choose instead to risk their horses. There have been horses ridden in classes despite severe injuries, even fractured bones. Drug testing has cut down on that, but it still happens. Some of the means used to get horses through the classes are hard to detect through a standard drug test, and some horses are tough and will try their best despite the pain.

But there is only one acceptable course to take when your horse is injured—do what is best for him, however long it takes. Quick fixes rarely work. Riding an injured horse can increase the injury. A good rider does not sacrifice his or her partner for a show, even if it is a big show. There will always be another show. Good horses are much harder to find.

Handling Nervousness

At the 1987 U.S. National Arabian and Half-Arabian Championships, I was so shaky with nerves that I had difficulty getting on the horse. My shirt collar squeezed like a noose around my neck and I felt like I would suffocate. My family had come with the horse, Firetok, a fourth of the way across the nation for me to ride. If I didn't make the cut in this first elimination round, it would all be for nothing. Firetok was a youngster of five in his first complete show season. Waiting for that first class to start, I was overwhelmed with doubts about both myself and him.

When I got on the horse, my anxiety seeped down into him and made him rigid with tension. When the gate opened his muscles were quivering from the stress. We were both a mess, and not too surprisingly made an error in the class.

We survived the cut anyway. After that I felt better and my nerves went away. Firetok and I then turned in some of the best performances of our career together. That was the year we won our first national championship.

It was a wonderful, exciting show for me, but my nervousness could easily have cost us the title.

Extreme nervousness can take the fun out of showing and damage your performance. Your nervousness strongly affects the horse. He is sensitive to you and can feel your tension. When you are nervous, he is more likely to make a mistake and you are more likely to ride badly. Many, many riders fail to achieve their dreams of great riding titles because they are unable to control their nervousness.

You might never get rid of your nervousness completely, but you can learn to handle it so it doesn't damage your enjoyment or performance. Be prepared for the show and your class well in advance. Nothing multiplies tension like thinking you might miss your class because you didn't start preparing early enough. Also, be organized. If you know where everything is before you need it, you're not going to work yourself into a panic and communicate that panic to your horse.

Know your horse and develop a confidence in him. When the anxiety starts rising up in your throat, tell yourself that you aren't doing this alone. The horse is your partner and knows what to do. This class is no different from what you have practiced hundreds of times. The better you know your horse, the easier it is to develop confidence in his abilities. You will know what he can or cannot handle.

If you have an adversarial relationship with your horse that prevents you from developing this confidence, you need a different horse.

It is equally as important to have confidence in yourself. You've practiced and you know what you are doing. You can handle anything that happens in the class. Concentrate on the horse and your job as the rider. This is the greatest single thing you can do to chase away nervousness and enhance your performance. With your attention absorbed by your duties as a rider, there is no space left for anything unrelated to the performance.

You also should ignore the attributes of your competitors in the ring. While it is good to recognize the abilities of your competitors, these become irrelevant once you enter the ring. Regardless of what the competition is doing, you must do your very best. Don't lose your confidence by thinking about how good someone else is.

Finally, adopt a positive, aggressive outlook in the face of adversity. Go in with the attitude that if your competitors want the title, they will have to get by you first.

Taking Care of Yourself

Caught in the hectic and exciting horse show atmosphere, it's easy to get overly tired, forget to eat, or overindulge in things that aren't good for you. Make some time in the schedule to take care of your basic needs—food, water and sleep. This is particularly important at the long shows, where exhaustion builds day after day.

Many riders take better care of their horses at shows than they do themselves. Don't skimp on the sleep you need. If classes run late into the night and don't give you enough time to sleep, try to find time during the day for a nap. When you are tired you are more likely to make mistakes or perform under par. Sleep deprivation slows down your thinking and responses, and impairs your judgment.

Skipping too many meals can do the same thing. As your blood sugar drops, so does your concentration and energy level. Try to eat at least one balanced meal a day while at a show. Pack nutritional snacks like apples for when you are hungry but can't take much time to eat. Drink a lot of fluids but avoid alcohol around class time. Alcohol erodes your balance, coordination, concentration and judgment. The more you drink, the worse you ride. And if you drink in excess, you may ride badly the next day as well because of a hangover.

Also avoid any kind of medication or drug that alters your perceptions, unless you need it for health reasons. This includes even over-the-counter items like strong cold medications that can make you feel drifty. If you believe the medication might interfere with your responses or concentration, don't take it until after your classes unless you have to. It is important at all times to be physically and mentally sharp in the ring.

WHAT YOU CAN DO RIGHT AWAY TO IMPROVE

- Put together lists of supplies needed for shows, then paste the lists in handy places.
- Put together a kit of crisis resolution items, such as a sewing kit, scissors, pins and black tape.
- Make an agreement with yourself to always put your horse's welfare first.

- Spend more time with your horse to get to know him better.
- Invest in some good cold and rain gear for yourself and the horse.

WHAT YOU CAN DO IN THE FUTURE

- Arrive early enough at shows to give yourself and the horse time to settle in.
- Allow ample time to prepare for the ring.
- Keep at-show practice sessions short.
- Make a conscious effort to defeat your nerves at each show.
- Pack nutritious snacks for the shows and try to take as good care of yourself as you do the horse.
- After every show, clean your clothes and horse supplies so that you won't have to stay up late the night before the show trying to get everything done.
- After the season is over, pack your clothes, grooming materials and other show supplies in a set place so when the new season starts you will not have to hunt for them.

Becoming Ring Wise

Entering the ring is the moment of truth. If you have done your work at home, it shows through in the quality of your performances.

To create the image of perfection you want the judge to see, you need to understand how to use the ring and your horse's abilities to your best advantage.

Many a good and diligent rider has lost a class because he or she failed to understand the mechanics of the show ring. The best horse doesn't always win the class. Sometimes the class goes instead to the rider who pushed the horse for his best and who always seemed to have him in just the right spot for the judge to see.

At small shows there is a commonly held belief that having a good ride means performing all the gaits upon request, making no major mistakes and getting the correct leads. That is not a good ride. It is the starting place.

A good ride is made up of the positive things you do, not the lack of negative things. It is the positive things that make a performance stand out favorably in a judge's mind. It is possible for a horse to make a major mistake and still win the class over horses that were error free, if that horse turned in an extraordinary performance.

Riding a class well requires some preparation and, once you are in the ring, concentration and an awareness of your surroundings. You must simultaneously push the horse for his best while keeping him in the best spot in the arena. It is a skill that takes practice and strategy.

PREPARATION

Before you go into a class, if possible watch one or more similar classes at the show. Note:

- *What style of horse is the judge picking?* For example, judges differ on just how they like to see a western horse's head placed. If you notice that the judge is picking predominately horses that have their noses way in, you probably can assume the judge likes horses shown in that fashion. Evaluate the performances of those who do well, and try to adjust your own accordingly if it makes sense to do so. These should not be major changes. They should be small things like going a little faster or slower.

  Never make drastic changes at a show. It will confuse the horse. If what the judge is selecting is greatly different from what you are doing, change nothing. Go to a couple more shows first and see what those judges want. You may have just hit upon an eccentric judge who is out of step with the times. But if after many shows you see that there is a consensus among the judges and you currently are not conforming, you may want to make that major change.

- *How are the riders entering the ring and which method works best?* Arenas come in all sizes and shapes. Whatever situation confronts you, you need to be able to go in without losing momentum or form. It looks bad for the horse as he enters the ring to break gait, fuss with his head or skip a stride. (Entering the arena will be discussed in detail later on in this chapter.)

- *Are there any obvious problem areas in the arena?* This might include wet spots, deep dirt, dips or discolored areas. In indoor arenas you may also want to look out for spots of sun. It is common for horses to shy at sun spots cast on the ground by roof vents. If you have the time, walk around the arena during a break to see what challenges it might offer.
- *Is there anything else that your horse might be afraid of in the arena?* Many show horses are practically fearless. They've been around so long and seen so much that a few arena decorations are not going to rattle them. But if you are on a timid horse, or a young horse, or you see something that could frighten even a veteran, make a mental note to stay clear of it.

Your final preparation is to mentally ready yourself for the ring. Before you ever enter the ring, ride the class in your mind. Plot how you will enter the ring, then see yourself doing it. Imagine yourself circling the arena, maneuvering your horse away from the crowds of horses so the judge sees only you. See yourself urging the horse into perfect form, the head tucked just right, the body compact, the gait ideal. See your own form perfect, sitting tall and elegant with legs and hands still. Mentally take yourself through all of the transitions, reversing and lining up, with everything done with the utmost flair and precision. Then imagine yourself being called out for first place, taking the ribbon, accepting the trophy and doing a victory pass.

The exercise will boost your confidence and potentially enhance your responses in the ring.

Adopt a positive, aggressive outlook even if you face adversity. Instead of thinking, "I don't have a chance against that horse," think, "I will have to make a supreme effort to compete against that horse." Being the underdog is not all that bad. It can inspire tremendous efforts. Regardless of whether I am riding what is considered to be the "best" horse or not, I strive to go into the ring with the attitude that if my competitors want the title, they will have to take it from me. They will not get it easily. I will not give it to them because I was so intimidated that I did not ride as well I could.

The "best" horse is the one that turns in the best performance on a given day. Average horses have extraordinary days. Good horses have bad days. The best horse in the ring is not always the one that is the most expensive, most talented or most beautiful. It is the horse that gives the best performance. As the rider it is up to you to make your horse the best. Don't let yourself be lulled by success into not working as hard as you should. When you put forth a halfhearted effort, so will the horse and your success will evaporate. And don't let low placings intimidate you into not trying to succeed. Give it your best effort every time and your placings will improve.

You may not always win, but by adopting this attitude you will be satisfied that you got the most the horse could offer, and that you rode well. That in itself is a worthy achievement.

When you get on the horse, he must become your sole focus. Merge with him. Center your mind on him, the way he feels, how he is responding to you, the rhythm of his movement. Listen to his breathing and feel his heart beating and the muscles moving beneath you. Watch his ears flick forward and back. With him at the center of your attention, everything that doesn't directly relate to the performance will disappear. From this absolute concentration can come your very best effort. Total, complete absorption in a task allows increased achievement.

Many athletes experience it as a narrowing down of their attention, like stepping into a tunnel. When your concentration is complete, you will barely notice the audience, or even if you are hot or cold. All that will exist for you is the horse, and to a lesser degree the ring and the other horses that share it with you. Don't let yourself be distracted. Push thoughts that don't directly relate to the performance out of your mind. They can wait until after the class. Allow yourself to be totally absorbed in the ring experience.

· ·

THE ENTRANCE

Your entrance offers the judge his or her first glimpse of you. This is your chance to grab and hold his or her attention favorably. Many judgments are made within those first few instants. In a large class, that first look may be when the judge decides if he or she is even going to watch you.

With that in mind, you want to be at your very best when you hit the ring. Don't just go in. Enter prepared. We're going to assume for discussion you are riding English Pleasure. It tends to present the most challenges going in because of the speed.

There often are a lot of horses crowded around the in-gate waiting to enter. If you enter right upon the tail of another horse, you have instantly lost the spacing you will need to be well seen by the judge. In whatever order you go in, make sure there is a lot of space—at least two to three horse lengths—between you and the person ahead of you. This is essential, but often overlooked even at large shows. Once, while waiting to go in the gate for a national class, a horse crowded so close behind mine that he literally stepped on my horse's tail. That's way too close.

Consider going in first if the opportunity presents itself. That is a favorite position for the bold rider because the rider and horse then make the first impression upon the judge's mind. The view of the pair also is uncluttered by other horses. You can get into the position to go in first by nudging your way through the crowd and making sure you are ready when the gate opens. But only go in if you are ready. How you look when you go in is more important than the order in which you go in.

It also is not worth going in first if you have to knock another horse out of the way to do it. That kind of behavior will quickly alienate your competitors. They may return your rudeness by doing the same thing to you.

Some riders prefer to go in last rather than first. It is your choice in what order you want to enter—first, last or somewhere in the middle. I do not believe the order makes a tremendous difference. One thing you do need to consider is what your horse would prefer. Most don't care about the order, but there are some horses that don't like to go in first. The surroundings are unfamiliar to them and there are no horses in there yet. Their uncertainty shows in their entrances. They look tentative and may lose their composure or shy.

When the gate opens, begin the gait you will be performing in the arena. In our example case of English Pleasure, it is the trot. Don't walk up to the gate, then start trotting once you get into the arena. You want to have a good, full-steam-ahead trot going before you even hit the ring. Remember, the judge's first glimpse of the horse should be when both you and the horse are looking your best. The horse looks better while engaged in a gait, rather than beginning the transition into the gait. You also tend to look best while the horse is solidly in a gait, rather than when you are cuing for a gait.

If you start your approach toward the gate and it doesn't feel right, stop before you get too close and try again. You can't do this indefinitely but while your competitors are going in you can make a second try at getting your horse ready, then ride him in last.

As you move through the gate, look up and pay attention to where you

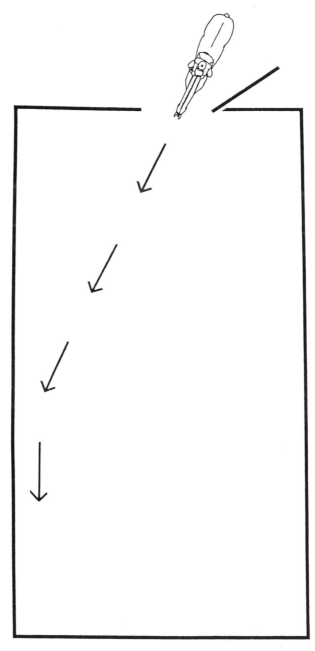

When you enter the arena, go in straight and angle over toward the rail, rather than turning to the rail immediately. A straight entrance looks more impressive and lessens the chance of the horse making an error, such as breaking gait.

are going. The arena probably is going to be rectangular or oblong. The gate usually is in the middle of a side, or the middle of the end. Going in, ignore the first corner. Rather than immediately swerving over to put yourself on the wall, head at an angle across the arena until you meet the wall (see illustration, page 118).

Corners are the most difficult part of ring work for the horse. They offer an increased chance that he will change speed, poke out his nose, skip or lose form in some other way. By going in at a straight line that angles over to the wall, you avoid the possible problems the first corner could have presented. Your entrance then is more likely to look good and be free of bobbles.

. . . .

RAIL WORK

You have three jobs in the ring—show the horse well, stay away from the clots of horses and avoid hazards.

If you've had lots of good practice sessions and instruction, you know what you need to do to make yourself and the horse look good. In equitation, use subtle cues and maintain your form throughout the class. In general, good equitation form requires you to pull your body erect and keep your hands and legs still. At the same time, maintain some suppleness to avoid looking stiff. Keep your heels down, eyes and chin up, and don't let your shoulders round forward. Follow the form for each equitation class as dictated in your rule book.

The horse should have solid form in equitation, but it is even more vital in pleasure. In general, the horse needs to maintain a consistent speed in each gait, perform each gait correctly and be collected so his body moves well and looks compact. He should be steady, keeping his composure and head set throughout all the gaits and transitions. He should also have an overall pleasing look to his performance, like it comes easily to him and he enjoys doing it. Regardless of the class, the horse should have a brightness to him, as if this is the most interesting thing he has done all day.

To help your horse maintain a pleasing look and prevent mediocre performances, there are a number of things you can do. First, limit his classes, as has been discussed in previous chapters. If he's exhausted, he's going to look and perform in an exhausted manner. It also helps to practice only very lightly at the shows, if at all. Practice is for home. He'd better know his stuff by the time you get to the show. If you do practice, do so outside the ring. Avoid taking him in the ring until class time. He then will show more interest and brightness because the surroundings will be new to him. The exception to this is horses that are skittish. Nervous horses tend to do better if they see the ring before their classes.

When in the class, really make the horse work. If you just sit on top and let him cruise through the class, he'll have time to get bored and act bored. Bump him with your legs when he needs it. Keep him collected, moving forward properly and looking good. Keep his nose in position. Be an aggressive rider, not a passive passenger. If you ride him well and thoughtfully, he will be absorbed by his work and it will show in a better performance.

Mediocrity shows itself in a lot of ways. Often the horse looks cranky, exhausted, lazy or bored. Crankiness is pretty common, especially by the end of a show. You can fight it some by trying to make the show easier on him, as has been discussed. Then when you get in the class, do your best to ride him well so he doesn't have time to think about how annoyed he is. He's going to give you a little harder time of it, but you can do it.

If he's truly exhausted, you should cancel the rest of his classes and go home unless there is an overriding reason to stay. There will be other shows.

The lazy and bored horse, on the other hand, needs you to be tougher with him. Ride him aggressively. Put your legs on him and make him go. Lazy horses and those bored with their work often shuffle along, dragging their hoofs, especially at the western jog. At the canter they cheat by adopting a gait that is half canter, half trot. Both will hurt your placings. You are going to have to work harder to win your ribbon. The bored horse also would do a little better if you did not take him into the ring until class time. The new surroundings will make the class more interesting for him, as has been discussed.

The horse turning in a mediocre performance often has an inconsistent head set that may bob or at times poke out. Usually the head set is at its worst during downward transitions, such as from a canter to a walk. The nose thrusts out and the horse stumbles into the walk because his weight has shifted forward and he is not using his body as he should. The same horse probably does a similar thing going from a walk into a canter. He flings his legs out and pops up his nose to try to get himself going.

Both problems are related to balance. He's not using his body in a coordinated, collected way, so he's making all these unnecessary movements to get the job done. These are things that should be worked out in practice at home with your trainer or instructor. A good performance is consistent, with the horse balanced and moving forward at all times, even through the transitions.

Throughout the class keep in mind your goal of an ideal performance, then try to meet it. You won't reach the goal all of the time, but it will help you focus on what you want out of the ride and eventually will improve your performance.

Make sure before starting any transition that the horse is prepared for it. When the announcer calls the next gait, you don't have to do it immediately. Take a moment to prepare the horse first. For example, let's say you are at the walk and the canter is called. If you do nothing more than cue him for the canter, he is more likely to get a wrong lead, fuss with his head and lose his form. You'll then spend a good amount of time trying to fix the problem under the eyes of the judge.

Taking just a moment to prepare him for the cue can avoid those hassles. Tighten your reins slightly, tense the muscles in your buttocks and down your legs to the knee. Leave the lower leg off him for the moment. The well-trained horse feels all of these things. It tells him, "Listen. A cue is coming." Make sure you have his attention. A horse that is listening to your signals will often flick one or both ears back and tense slightly.

You need the horse's attention before you ask for the gait. If he is not paying attention—if, for instance, he's staring off in the distance at something—bump him lightly with your legs. Then, when you have his attention, give him the cue with your lower leg. He should go into the gait in a nice, collected, precise manner that will put you in good standing for the rest of the work in that gait.

Notice these instructions for the transition didn't say to feed him a bunch of rein. A common mistake riders make when asking a horse to go into a faster gait is giving the horse a lot of slack. Although it seems logical, it leads to problems.

Training teaches a horse to perform in a balanced manner with a rider on his back. You direct his collection and balance with your legs and the reins, and he's been taught to rely on that and respond to it.

When you give him a lot of slack in asking for the canter, you are taking away one of the balance points and increasing the chance he's going to start badly. Most horses need at least a little bit contact to help them balance, collect and prepare for the gait. The exception are the finely tuned western horses often seen competing at high levels. They are ridden with the reins hanging quite loose through the entire class. The horse's collection comes from his extensive training and from the rider's leg and body cues. Until your horse can enter a gait without moving his nose out or losing collection, he needs you to tighten the reins a little during the transitions.

The mechanics of all upward transitions are the same. Gather the reins back a little, tense slightly, ensure his attention, then ask for the gait. With the canter, feel for the way he shifts his weight as he goes into the gait. Someday after years of riding you will know from that weight shift which lead the horse is going to take before his first stride of canter strikes the ground.

The downward transitions (from the canter to the walk, for example) are similar to the upward transitions. Preparation is involved in both. Don't just throw your weight back, stiffen your legs and pull on the reins. That makes the horse come down heavy on his front end instead of using his hind quarters. It may also make him open his mouth or throw his head. The whole thing looks sloppy.

Use your entire body to bring the horse down in his transitions. Pull your stomach muscles in, tuck your tail bone and drop your weight down hard through your buttocks onto the horse's back. Pretend you are trying to push right through his body to land on the ground beneath his belly. Simultaneously, tighten the reins slightly. That should be all you need to do for a nice transition. As he reaches the gait you wish, bump him lightly with your legs to move him forward into it, even if it's just the walk. Use the weight cue every time in practice and the horse will understand and respond to it in the ring.

It is all right in the ring to use verbal cues to aid your transition, but they should be quiet, infrequent and backed by body cues. Clicking once or twice to encourage the trot is okay. But clicking incessantly is annoying, leaves a bad impression and encourages the horse to ignore the sound. When you use a verbal cue that is a word, like "whoa" or "walk," remember also to be consistent in how you say it. If your tone or inflection changes too much, the horse will not recognize the word.

In practice, when you use a verbal cue insist the horse respond to it immediately. For example, when you click once or twice he should move forward into the gait with energy—immediately. When he responds appropriately, don't use the sound or word again until you need it.

The same is true with all cues. It is important to insist every time that the horse respond immediately upon feeling or hearing it. It is not acceptable, for example, for a horse to trot into the canter, unless the horse is very green and just learning his cues. The experienced horse knows what you want. A sluggish response means he's not paying attention or is feeling lazy. When he does that, kick your cue leg or legs into his sides as hard as you can, then check him back, make him walk a short distance and ask him again, gently. He should pick the gait up right away. If he doesn't, do the exercise with a whip or spurs until he understands that the cue means "right now."

If it is necessary to strike him, hitting him once is sufficient to get your point across. Any more than that is unnecessary. The same is true of the spurs. If he responds sluggishly, kick the spur into his side—once. Hitting or kicking him many times will not make him learn the lesson any faster.

. . . .

PLACEMENT IN THE RING

Nearly as essential to having a good ride in the ring is making sure the judge knows it's good. He or she has to see you to place you favorably. That means staying out of the crowds and keeping your horse in the clear as long as possible (see illustrations, pages 124 and 125). This happens by design, not accident. Aware of your surroundings, you will be watching constantly for opportunities to better display the horse. You do not need to be a permanent fixture on the rail throughout the class. You can move around, cut across, cut corners and go deep in corners. You can also move on and off the rail. If you feel the need, you can ride the whole class in from the rail.

The following are situations that occur in the ring, with ways to meet the challenges they present. As you read through them, imagine yourself in the situations. The exercise will help you learn more about using the show ring to your advantage.

You are on the rail at a canter, completely surrounded by other horses. There is one immediately in front of you, one behind and several alongside (see illustration, page 126). *You want to free yourself from the pack. What should you do?*

This is what the judge sees when he or she looks at riders on the rail. The outside horse is covered up. Remember that for a judge to place you well, you have to be seen. Work to stay in the clear.

You have several options. The smoothest is to go very deep in the next corner. The crowd will pass you by.

You also could slow the horse's canter slightly without breaking gait. Again, the crowd will pass you by. As soon as the horse behind you has passed by, resume your former speed and cut across the arena to a clear area. This maneuver will rid you of the pack faster, but it is riskier than the first.

You are completely surrounded by horses when suddenly one of them begins bucking. If you don't do something fast, you will become entangled in that rider's problems. What should you do?

Get away as quickly as possible without breaking gait. You cannot wait for a corner or slow down to create space. Collect your horse up, put your legs on him and push him through one of the little spaces between the horses, even if it looks like a tight fit. The faster the gait you are in, the more difficult this becomes, but it is possible even at the canter. You may brush the other horses and risk breaking gait, but it is your best chance to emerge unscathed. Once you get free, cut across the arena.

Way ahead of you a horse is shaking his head and beginning to misbehave. Should you do anything?

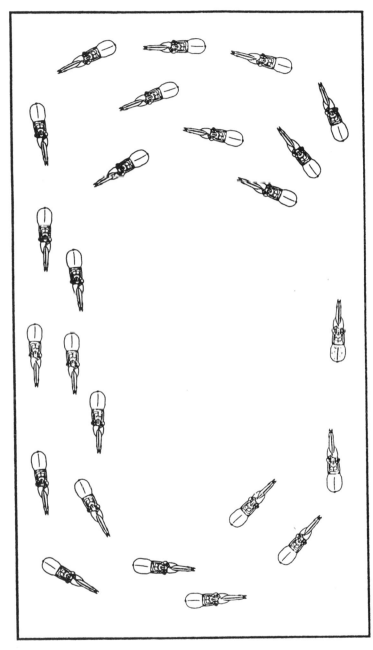

If you were the judge standing in the middle of this class, who could you see the best? Of all the horses, the gray has the best position. Although you could see all the horses on the inside track, the view is cluttered against a backdrop of other horses. And some of the horses buried deep in groups would be hidden from sight entirely. Illustration by Shirley Dickerson and the author.

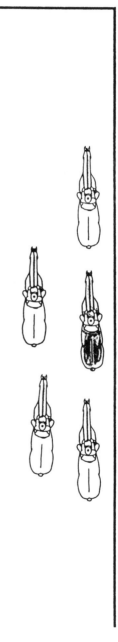

You are riding the gray horse, and know that in this position the judge cannot see you. Your best strategy for escape is to take the coming corner extremely deep, and let the crowd pass you by. Illustration by Shirley Dickerson and the author.

Yes. Cut across a corner to get ahead of the horse or take a deep corner to put more distance between you and the horse. The small problem he is having now could turn into a large problem. You want to be as far from him as possible so you are not disrupted. Plan ahead.

Your horse moves a little faster than some in the class. On the rail, you come up behind a group of horses. What should you do?

Take your corners deep to distance yourself from the group. If you get close to the group before you reach the corner, pull off the rail to position yourself to pass them. Then cut the next corner to put yourself way ahead of them. Don't wait to act until your horse's nose is almost bumping the rump in front of you. If you wait, your horse may break gait. The worst thing to do is stop or change gaits to get back your spacing.

You are having a nice, smooth ride when suddenly a horse cuts in front of you, nearly hitting your horse in the face with a tail. How can you escape without breaking gait?

Quickly take a stronger hold on the reins, put your legs on the horse's sides and maneuver him off the rail (see illustration, page 128). The faster the gait you are working in, the faster you are going to have to react to keep your horse from breaking or raising up his head. Maneuver around the other horse. The rider isn't very aware, so you might want to stay clear of him or her through the rest of the class.

You are in the western jog on the rail when a horse that was to your forward inside starts floating back to the rail. The competitor's horse's rump is about even with your horse's shoulder, and you don't think the rider has even noticed you are there. If he continues on course, he will bump your horse and probably cause you to stop. Since you already are moving at an extremely slow speed, it will not be possible for you to slow enough for him to get by without disrupting you. How should you deal with this?

Tell him you are there. Say repeatedly, loud enough for him to hear, "Rail." That tells him you are on the rail and he is too close.

You are riding a little horse in a class of giants. How can you make sure he will be seen?

Size is immaterial to an impressive performance that will catch the judge's eye. Many great horses are small. There are some things you can do, however, to make his small stature less noticeable. Ride him a little to the inside of the rail. To the eye of the judge who is standing in the middle of the ring, the horse will appear slightly larger because the horse is closer to him than those

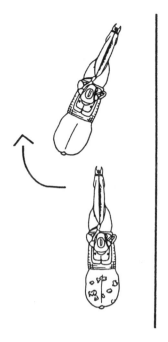

You are riding the Appaloosa when another horse cuts you off. To avoid breaking gait, take a stronger hold of your horse, put your legs on him and veer sharply around your competitor. Illustration by Shirley Dickerson and the author.

on the rail. Stay away from the largest horses in the class if you can. When you line up, take your time and let most of the other horses go in the lineup first, then park by the smallest one you see.

You are in an intensely crowded class. How can you best be seen?

This is a difficult one. In classes like this, the bulk of the riders will ride way to the inside of the rail, getting closer and closer to the judge in an effort to be seen. That means there are so many people riding on the inside that adding yourself to the masses isn't going to win you much exposure. Neither will riding on the rail, because the judge's vision is obscured by the many horses circling on the inside.

Your best bet for being noticed, of course, is a brilliant performance. But other than that you can help yourself be seen by using a variety of placements.

Take a few laps on the rail and a few to the inside. When you take the inside position, go completely inside, allowing no one between you and the judge. Cut across once or twice, as if to gain better spacing. It's not wise to do this too much, but it can help you be seen. Also, take your time lining up, and if the opportunity presents itself, line up directly in front of the judge. But make sure you don't get so close he or she has to step back. Both in lining up and in rail work, getting too close makes a bad impression.

You are riding a young horse that becomes nervous when other horses get close. How do you lessen the chance he will blow up?

Keep him away from the other horses as much as possible and ride him off the rail. Riding to the inside increases your ability to get him out of situations where horses might get too close.

As you travel along the rail, you notice a group of horses is coming up on you. What should you do?

Your action will depend on the speed of their approach. If they are moving fairly fast, do nothing and they will pass you by. But if their rate of speed is similar to your own, you need to get away from them or you will become enmeshed in the crowd. Take a deep corner to place yourself way behind them.

You are riding on the inside track of a pack of horses. Should you remain there?

If this is a crowded class and you have the very inside track, stay there for the time being. There is no one between you and the judge's eye. But if there is a nice open space on the rail you will want to cut a corner or cut across the ring to put yourself there. Your horse will look better against a blank background than against the backdrop of many horses.

There is a horse in your class that you believe is more gifted than yours. Will this have an impact upon where you place yourself in the arena?

Yes. If possible, avoid riding near the talented horse. He will probably still win, but in some cases you may enhance your placing by staying away from him. It is better to ride near horses that are less talented than yours. Judging is an art of comparing one horse to another. There's no reason to point out your horse's shortcomings by putting him on the rail next to an extremely talented horse.

Regardless of the situations you find yourself in, following four basic principles will help you achieve the best placement in the ring and avoid problems:

1. Look up so you can see what is ahead of you.
2. Be aware of what is happening around you so you can anticipate potential problems and areas opening up on the rail.
3. Take advantage of openings to give the judge a clear view of your horse.
4. Use circles sparingly if at all. It is better to gain spacing by cutting a corner or taking a deep corner. Those two moves are the smoothest. You can also cut across the ring if need be.

While many riders make circles to gain spacing, circles often lead to errors. It is more difficult for a horse to perform a circle than a line. Every time you perform a circle, you risk the horse breaking gait or losing form. The faster the gait and smaller the circle, the greater the risk of bobbles. And because the other horses in the ring are moving, it is easy to misjudge distances and end up placing your horse in another crowd of horses instead of in the open space you were aiming for.

. . . .

AVOIDING HAZARDS

The show ring can have a surprising number of hazards. Be on guard against anything that might disrupt your ride.

Hazards come in many forms. During your preparation you may have spotted one or two and in your ring work will avoid them. But always be on the lookout for unforeseen hazards. The more timid or inexperienced your horse, the more you need to be watchful. The iron horse, one that thinks of himself as clad in armor, may not care if a can of soda pop falls off the rail into the arena in front of him. Then again, he may feel the need to jump over it. Even with the iron horse, be aware of your surroundings and try to avoid problems.

Potential hazards include the audience, ring decorations, bad footing and your competitors. Competitor hazards include things such as a horse near you misbehaving. Be vigilant and distance yourself from him. Also be on the lookout for problems coming from the audience. At some large shows, people scream, whistle, clap, stomp and yell during the class. It depends on the type of breed show you are attending as to how prevalent this is. Experienced horses ignore this and some even like it, but yours may find it disruptive until he gets used to it. Ride him a bit to the inside to lessen the impact of the sound on him.

The audience can also cause you difficulties in other ways. Most of the problems are unavoidable because they occur spontaneously, but if you see a potential problem steer clear of it. For example, if you see a child roaring a toy truck along the outside of the rail, or someone fussing with an umbrella and about to open it, give a wide berth.

Also swing wide of any show ring decorations that you think might be frightening to the horse. The bigger the show, the fancier these are going to be. Sometimes they're a little scary, especially for the inexperienced horse. If he appears truly frightened by something, keep your distance from it if you can without disrupting your rail work. You gain nothing by forcing him near it in the class. He will likely lose his fear of it as the class progresses. During the break, you may want to walk him near it to ease his fears.

In the ring be particularly wary of curtains. These are often placed on the rail to cover up something or provide a backdrop for photos. Give them a berth of a few feet when you go by. The breeze created by your passing often makes them move.

The final hazard to look out for is bad footing. Rocks, mud, slick spots and deep spots in the arena can hurt your ride. Your horse can stumble, slip or sustain an injury. Stay clear of the problem areas you spotted during your preparation. If the arena is extremely rocky, see if you can get the show to organize a rock-picking party before the classes start. Volunteer to help. Rocks are a hazard to your horse's soundness.

. . . .

FACIAL EXPRESSIONS

Some riding instructors coach their students to wear wide smiles throughout every class. A nice smile does complement the ride, but unfortunately few people can maintain that kind of smile throughout an entire class. As the class progresses, the smiles begin to look strained, false and can even become tension-induced grimaces. They then detract from the image the rider was trying to project.

Most people in high-level competition do not smile. Instead they wear expressions of intense concentration. They have no time to think about smiling.

If smiling seems forced to you, don't smile. Your facial expression will be much more pleasant if you aren't forcing it. Concentrate on your riding instead of your face. Save your smiles for when they come naturally, such as when the judge compliments your horse.

On the other hand, if you have a nice, natural smile that comes easily to your face, use it to your advantage in the ring. You do not have to wear it constantly, but a frequent, pleasant smile can portray to the judge your enjoyment in riding and in your horse.

. . . .

PATTERNS

Many equitation classes are won or lost based on how well the pattern or other test is performed. It is one of the things that separates the good riders from the best riders.

Many classes require that the pattern be posted beforehand. It's usually stapled up near the ring or at the office. Find and read it. Make sure you know it and understand it well. If you have questions, ask them when the judge calls for questions prior to the start of the patterns.

If you are at a show approved by the American Horse Shows Association (or in Canada, the Canadian Equestrian Federation), and you have read your rule book, you already know what the judge can and cannot ask for. All of tests the judge can ask for are listed in the AHSA book under "Equitation." The judge can request one of the tests listed, or string a number together to form a pattern. In English Equitation, the judge can even ask for you to swap horses with a competitor for a short time, but that's usually only seen in the highest forms of competition.

Once you know what is in the rule book, there is no need to get nervous about what the judge will ask for. You can practice all of the tests at home to make sure you and the horse can do them easily. Tests should be done with precision, each movement crisp and deliberate.

The patterns require planning, whether they include circles, straight lines or a serpentine. Among the most common problems riders have with patterns is that they get lost. They can't remember where the center to the figure eight was or how big the last circle was compared to the next. Sometimes they lose count of lead changes or other moves.

To avoid this, map out the pattern in your mind's eye before you start. Look around the arena for things you can use as landmarks.

For example, let's say you've been asked to perform two figure eights. Look for a landmark around the ring that you can use to note where the center of your eights will be. The landmark could be anything—a post, a sign on the wall, a flag hanging at the end of the arena. When you start your pattern, you will line yourself up with that and return to that exact spot after each circle of your eights. That will ensure the center of your pattern staying in one place.

You may also want to pick out landmarks to make sure your circles are round and of the same size. It's easy in the midst of riding a circle to lose track of how large it has become, or how it compares to the last one you did. On either side of the spot you have picked for the center, look for landmarks that you can use for the outer edge of the circles. It will make your circles round and of equal size with each other.

Using landmarks will keep you from getting lost while doing the pattern. Concentrate fully on what you are doing. If you are asked for two circles, count them as you go around to make sure you don't accidentally do three. Follow instructions exactly. If the judge asks for changes of speed during the pattern, make your speed changes obvious.

Don't try to force the horse to do something he is untrained for. If your horse doesn't know how to do flying lead changes, ask him for simple changes (breaking down from a canter to a trot, then picking up the opposite lead). If the judge asks for a wall run with a sliding stop and your horse has never done one before, just canter down the wall and do a normal stop. That is much better than running the horse then jerking on his mouth to try to make him stop fast.

Stick to what you know the horse can handle within the requirements of the pattern. The ring is not the place to try something new. When you try to force him to do something he does not understand and has never done before, it shows. You are more likely to lose points that way than riding him through the pattern conservatively.

Prepare him for everything you ask for, just as you prepared him for the transitions during the rail work. Many errors come simply because the horse was caught by surprise. For example, some judges like to ask riders, one at a time, to canter from the lineup in a specific lead in a straight line. The difficulty comes because a horse standing in line thinks he's done working. He may not be paying as much attention. And some don't like to leave the other horses in the line.

The rider who just gives the horse the canter cue is likely to get a poor response. The horse may just side away from the leg, pop up his nose or go crooked into a canter. The rider may lose form when the horse's sluggish response calls for desperate measures, like repeatedly kicking him.

Prepare the horse and save yourself some grief. You don't have to rush forward to do the test. Take a moment, prepare him for it, then do it. Collect your reins, tense your body and brush him with your legs. It tells him something is coming.

It is hard to go from a standstill into a canter performed in a straight line. But it becomes fairly easy if you know a little trick. The first cue you give is not for the canter. It's for the walk. After you prepare the horse, cue him for the walk. Then as he completes his first stride forward, cue him for the canter. He will pick it up much more easily and stay in a straighter line than had you asked for the canter first. To the observer, it merely looks like the horse was moving forward to the canter.

. . . .

FIXING PROBLEMS IN THE RING

The worst possible place for a problem to occur is in a show ring. Unfortunately, it does happen occasionally, and you have to deal with it as best you can. The problems fall into three categories—major errors, horse problems and natural disasters like throwing a shoe in the ring.

The natural disasters are usually easy to deal with. Under AHSA rules, the rider can call a time out to fix the problem. Just ride to the center and ask the ring steward for a time out. Time-outs are usually used to correct tack problems like tightening a loose cinch or fixing a broken chin strap. You can request up to two time-outs in a class as long as the total time does not surpass five minutes. You also can call two people into the ring to help you fix the problem, if necessary.

If your horse loses a shoe, the clock doesn't start ticking on your time-out until the farrier touches the shoe or enters the ring, whichever comes first.

If the problem can't be fixed in your allotted time, you have the option of riding the class or excusing yourself.

These rules are in effect at every AHSA-rated show you attend. The rules do vary a little from breed to breed, so if you are attending specific breed shows you may want to read up on what your breed allows.

The unrated shows generally allow time-outs, though the shows do not have to follow AHSA rules.

Much harder to handle than the natural disasters are the major errors. They are the errors that are so bad there is no way to fix them. Once the major error is committed, your best option is to make the rest of your ride exemplary. Becoming angry at the horse is a waste of time. Concentrate instead on what you will do next. There is a chance that the rest of your performance will outshine your error and you will do well in spite of it.

There is also a chance the judge didn't see the error. This does happen occasionally. The worst error I have ever experienced in the show ring went totally ignored by the judges. Either they didn't see it or liked the performance well enough to place me anyway.

The class was at the U.S. National Arabian and Half-Arabian Championship horse show. It was a qualifier to determine the Top 20 horses in the nation, who then would compete for the Top 10, and then for the championship title. The horse, Bey Liza, and I had gone hundreds of miles to be there. The class was extremely crowded. Liza hated crowds. The class was trotting the first direction when a horse came up so close behind Liza that they nearly brushed.

Liza kicked him in the face. I heard her shoe connect with the horse's bit. That horse jerked away, slammed into another, and caused all sorts of mayhem among the horses around us. Liza broke into a canter. I was horrified and shaken. But since it really couldn't get much worse from there, I tried to gather up my wits and make the rest of the ride the best I could. Other than the error, it was a good go. Naughty Liza and I won Top 20, and went on to higher competition.

Don't assume that because you have made an error the class is over. It may not be. You may be able to salvage it. The worst thing you can do is let the error rattle you. Sometimes the error will drop you out of the ribbons, but not all the time.

The exception to this rule of trying to make the best of things is if the problem is so bad you feel you should not continue, or if the horse's behavior is a hazard to you or your competitors. This would be something like the horse constantly acting up. Excuse yourself from the ring. Work on the problem in the warmup arena or at home. Extremely bad behavior is not something that should be worked on in the show ring.

If the bad behavior is something that only occurs in the show ring, enter a few scantily populated classes and make the horse complete them. Don't worry about placing or how you appear to the judge. Discipline the horse in the ring. The goal is for the horse to learn you are not going to tolerate that kind of behavior. He will quickly learn that he can't get away with bad behavior in the ring.

But remember that for punishment to be effective, it must be done within instants of the error. If you cannot punish him within that time, don't do it at all.

If the horse has been generally bad, you may want to take him into the warmup arena after the class and continue to ride until he improves. However, anger has no place in these sessions. Some people become so angry with a horse that after the class they abuse him. The horse is ridden into a lathered sweat and struck and jerked repeatedly. Since the error has long passed, these kind of sessions teach the horse nothing except fear. He is not mentally capable of connecting the abuse with his bad behavior in the ring.

Small problems that occur in the ring can often be fixed quietly without risking your placings or doing anything extreme. Sometimes you can remedy the problem before the judge notices you're having trouble.

The key to fixing the problem is to do it as early as possible. Often you can feel the horse starting to think about bad behavior. You may feel him begin to tense, round his back a little, hollow out his back, give his head a little shake, or lean on the bit. Listen to the horse for these little clues. They are the beginning of later problems.

The tense horse and the one rounding his back may be thinking about bucking, changing leads or breaking gait. The horse giving his head a shake could be having similar thoughts if he seems in a playful mood. In all three cases, check the horse back to remind him he needs to stay in form.

Another possible reason for him shaking his head is that he's mad. Before you act, think about possible sources of his anger. Are you holding the reins too tight, being rough with them or letting your legs brush carelessly against his sides? Hands and legs are for cues. Keep them still except when giving a cue. To relieve the horse's irritation, lighten up on the reins, and quiet your legs. If he seems angry about having too many horses too close to him, try to get him in the clear. He is best seen there anyway. If he's just being cranky, bump with your legs. The shaking of the head in that case was bad behavior you shouldn't tolerate.

The horse that hollows out his back has another problem. While it's possible he has a sore back, its more likely he's losing collection. With some horses, you can feel this hollowing. With others, it feels like the horse is getting longer. Either way, the horse is losing the nice, compact form important for all performance classes. The horse leaning on the bit is often headed for loss of collection, too. As he dumps some of his weight forward, his hindquarters pop out behind him, leaving him uncollected. He is also likely to lose his head set.

You've got to fix this when you first feel him begin to do it. You can fix it on the fly or in a transition. Try to find a spot in the ring where your repair work won't be obvious.

For example, let's say you have a hunter that likes to lean on the bit. As the class progresses, you can feel him getting heavier and heavier on your hands, and you know from past experience that by the middle of the class he will be pulling so hard you won't be able to keep him collected and his nose tucked. You need to tell him this is not acceptable, but you don't want to do something so obvious that you will jeopardize your placing.

The best place to fix a problem is where the judge can't see you—behind him or her. You want to push the horse hard with your legs into the bit. When you cross behind the judge, kick your horse hard once or twice in the ribs and check back on the reins. Make him give to the bit and respond to your legs. If you have a snaffle, break the horse's pressure on it by pulling the head to the side with one rein, then straightening it when the horse gives.

If there is no place where the judge can't see—which is often the case with multi-judge systems—you have two options. You can try to maneuver so that another horse is between you and the judges, then do your fixing. Or you can do it in a corner. The corner is in full view of the judges, but the curve sometimes aids in resolving the problem. For example, the head of the pushy hunter could be pulled strongly to the side during the corner as you squeeze your legs hard into his sides. It would look natural, but would also help back him off the bit. Corners can be good places to work on head sets and collection.

Gait transitions are also good places to work on the horse. Each gait brings the opportunity to make it better or worse than the last. You are starting over. Push your horse up to the bit and make him give to it as you drop down to a slower gait, or right before you begin a faster gait.

The transitions are helpful as well for when you're not having serious problems but horse's performance has been less than it could be. You can use the transitions to spruce him up for the next gait. It is a matter of preparation. At each transition, use the change of speed to get the horse collected and listening, as has been discussed. Use your legs to push for several strides to start out each gait, regardless of whether it is a faster or slower gait. Remember, there is as much need for collection in the walk as the canter.

REVERSING

There's no one right way to reverse the horse. As long as it is done smoothly, you can choose the method of your choice—circling toward the middle, circling toward the wall, pivoting on the front or hindquarters, or cutting across the ring.

The one important point you should be aware of is that most horses go better one direction than the other. Horses come in right and left "handed," just like people. This is more apparent in some horses than others. The horse's preference is particularly easy to see when he's a youngster learning his leads. He will tend to prefer one lead over the other.

As a mature horse in the show ring, he will give you the lead you request, but that does not mean he has lost his preference. He will remain right or left sided. It may influence his performance, making him go better one way than the other. He may also tend to have more problems one way than the other.

As the rider, it is helpful for you to know which direction is his weakest. When going that direction, help him along a little more with your hands and legs to keep him collected. You may want to make your cues stronger too, and give him a little extra time to prepare for the gaits.

On his good direction, you can put a little more pressure on him. He is at his most capable this direction and can show the judge his very best.

. . . .
LINING UP

The last place you are judged is in the lineup. When the announcer calls for you to go in, do so fairly promptly. Dally too long and you risk annoying the judge. In some classes such as Park, it is common for the competitors to make several laps after the lineup is called. Each is trying to make a winning last impression on the judge. It gets to be excessive. Line up when the lineup is called. If you are not in a good spot to line up when it is called, continue around until you are better positioned to go in. It is all right to make one last pass to impress the judge, but don't make more than one.

In the line, the horse's body should be straight and in a nice straight line with all the other horses. If the judge is asking horses in line to back, get your horse ready for the command before the judge reaches you. When asked to back, take a moment to prepare the horse. You don't have to back immediately. The moment you take to prepare will pay off in a better back. Shift your weight back, touch the reins and put your legs on him. Your legs give direction and help him back straight. Don't look behind him. When you look around your weight shifts and he backs crooked. Keep your weight in the middle.

In the line, make your horse keep his form—body compact, nose tucked. Don't let him rest a foot, hang his head or fidget. Reprimand him with your legs for any of these things. The absence of pressure is a reward. If you do nothing, he'll think his behavior is good.

Remember that in the line you are still being judged. After the card is in, all judging has stopped, and it is all right to talk to your competitors and move your horse out of the lineup. If the horse is hot and sweating and it is taking a while for the placings to be announced, you may want to walk him around to cool. Just make sure the judge's card is in before you leave the line.

Once the judge's card is in, it is all right to relax somewhat, but do not let yourself or the horse fall apart. The official judging for this class may be over, but you are still in the ring. The audience is watching and so may be the judge. It is important to maintain a good impression.

ACCEPTING THE RIBBON

Accept your placing gracefully regardless of what it is.

When you place low, be polite and leave the ring in your horse's best gait. Strive to make the judge wonder why he or she didn't place you higher. Even if you thought you should have done better, don't make a fuss in the ring by refusing the ribbon, throwing it to the ground or letting your displeasure show. The only impression you will make is that you are a bad sport.

When you win, smile and enjoy the victory, but don't get arrogant about it. It is wonderful to win. It is not wonderful for your head to get so puffed up that you are unbearable to the people around you. No one is invincible. No matter how much someone wins, he or she also loses sometimes. Be confident but don't let it run away with you.

When you ride badly but win anyway, just enjoy the victory and pretend you earned it. The ring isn't the place to smirk, joke or say how shocked you are. It's not a good idea to make some comment that might lead the judge to reconsider his or her opinion of you and your horse. That judge is going to see you again in another class.

If the award you receive in a class seems cumbersome or something your horse might be afraid of, tell the presenter you would like to pick it up in the office following the class. It is better to pick up the award up later than to risk dropping it or losing control of the horse.

It is also wise not to allow the ribbon to be clipped to the horse's bridle unless you are certain he is not going to object. The ribbons fluttering by his eye can be frightening or irritating to him. Try it first at home before attempting it in the show ring.

WHAT YOU CAN DO RIGHT AWAY TO IMPROVE

- Practice handling show ring crowding situations with a group of other riders. You may want to try on horseback a number of the situations listed under "Placement in the Ring."
- Read the patterns listed under "Equitation" in the AHSA rule book and give some of them a try.
- Determine whether your horse is right or left sided. You can do this by watching him play loose. He will tend to choose one lead more than the other. You are also likely as a rider to notice his preferences. Going his favorite direction, he may feel more fluid or take commands a little more readily.

WHAT YOU CAN DO IN THE FUTURE

- In practice and in the show ring, always prepare your horse before you ask for a gait.
- Cultivate an increased awareness of your surroundings in the ring.
- Strive to be an aggressive rider whose ride demands the most from the horse.
- Watch how accomplished riders use the ring to their best advantage.

CHAPTER 9

Through the Judges' Eyes

Your placing in a class is determined not only by the judge at center ring, but also by every judge who has ever stood in a ring.

Through their decisions, judges promote or discourage new trends, refine the qualities of each class, and speak to the proper type and build of every breed of horse. They determine what is and is not a good performance, and a good horse.

They are also the educators. They offer you the chance to sharpen your skills and measure yourself and the horse against other horses and riders. And by watching how judges place the other classes, you can also learn a great deal about desirable qualities in performances, riders and horses.

If you have the chance, talk to the judge after the last class. Many judges are willing to speak with riders once classes are over. Questions you could ask might include: Why did you place me the way you did? What were the qualities of the winning rider that won him or her the placing? What are you looking for in a horse and rider in this kind of class? What were the strongest points about my performance? What were the weakest points? What are my strongest points as a rider? What are my weakest? What are my horse's strongest points? What are his weakest? In practice, what areas should I concentrate on the most? What other suggestions can you offer to help me improve?

Try to get the judges to be as specific as possible when you speak to them. It will further your education. Most judges have spent their lives working with horses. They have judged hundreds of classes and seen some of the best horses and riders in the country. They have a great deal of insight, experience and knowledge to share.

The following are interviews with some of the nation's top judges, talking about qualities they want to see in the ring and what tips they would offer you as a rider.

. . . .

HAL ARMSTRONG

Armstrong has been an American Quarter Horse Association–approved judge since 1977 and has judged the AQHA World Championship Quarter Horse Show. He and his wife, Jan, also raise and show Quarter Horses.

First impressions are critical. I watch the horses as they come in, and follow them about halfway around the arena. If they show me something I like, then I'm going to spend more time watching them. By the time they've been around a couple times, I've begun picking my first-, second- and third-place horses, as well as the horses I'm not going to use.

I'm not trying to find mistakes. I'm looking for the pluses.

Common mistakes made by some riders are that they lose concentration. They lose track of why they are there, and it shows in their performance.

They also often use aids that are way too noticeable. They need to practice imperceptible aids. I don't like to see them lean over and kick the horses to get into a lope. They should maintain their position at all times, especially in the transitions. When you see a few things bad like that, and there are several dozen horses in the ring, you tend to fall away from looking at that one.

I like to see riders relaxed, but with an air of confidence. If you come in and you look like you are there to win, that will transmit to the judge. I can tell if riders are worried. When they start to get nervous, they'll lean over, they'll start getting tense, their hands may come up and they will start looking down. I don't penalize people for that in pleasure classes, but it all goes together. You're not going to get a relaxed performance out of the horse if the rider is tense.

The most important thing you can do to improve yourself is watch the winners and get help from someone who is qualified. So many times people want to save a few bucks, so go to an instructor who is cheaper instead of to the one they need. That can delay your progress.

The next most important thing to do, especially for horsemanship and equitation riders, is to read the rule book. I see a lot of riders who just need to read the rule book more closely. They should be absolutely certain they know what the right position is in both Hunt Seat Equitation and Western Horsemanship and try to stay in it. They also need to follow the pattern exactly as it is posted.

It really hurts me when I see riders who have good horses, but don't know how to sit the horses properly. They have the horses to get the job done, but they haven't taken the time to practice or maybe gotten the proper instruction. The rule book says, for example, that in Western Horsemanship you should have a straight line through your ear, the center of the shoulder, the center of the hip and the back of the heel. That is as basic as it gets. You just have to practice it until you have it perfected.

I've seen some riders come in on horses that that are not as experienced as others, but the riders are outstanding in their position. Those riders are going to score high in Horsemanship and Huntseat Equitation classes.

In Western Pleasure, I want a horse with ring presence. He should look like he knows what he is doing and perform the gaits properly. The best western horses are good movers, are well cadenced in the jog, collected in the lope and maintain consistent speed. They should not speed up or slow down in the corners or straightaways.

There are some very specific guidelines now for how Quarter Horse pleasure horses should move. The tip of the ears should not be below the level of the withers, they shouldn't be flexed behind the bit or have their nose stretched out, and they shouldn't look lethargic (see illustration, page 145). The horse should look alert and work on a reasonably loose rein.

With the hunter horses, I want them to be able to walk on. I don't want a pit-a-pat walk. I want to see them cover the ground at the walk. At the trot, I like to see a long, low, cadenced, ground-covering trot. The neck should be level and the face perpendicular or slightly forward. They should have light contact on the bit and not be flexed behind it.

The canter should be collected, and if a hard gallop is called for, there should be a lengthening of stride rather than just more speed. Collection is vital in all classes and at every gait.

Ring position is also very important. The judge must be able to see you. Use your corners to improve your position by cutting or going deep so the judge can see you by yourself, in the clear. Good position is something that comes with experience, but you need to be aware that it is important.

Regardless of the class, the riders and horses need to be well groomed and have tack and clothing that fits and is contemporary. In the Quarter Horse ring today, you just don't come in with an old buckstitched outfit. It just shows you are not up to date.

The horse should also be fit and well cared for. A good conditioning, worming and hoof care program is essential. It's important as well to spend a lot of time

Poor Western Pleasure form commonly seen in the ring is to let the horse's poll drop below his withers and pull his nose in too far. This horse's head should be up higher, and the nose not quite so deeply tucked.

This rider displays good Saddleseat Equitation form with her head up, body erect, heels down. The rider's shoulders are directly over the hip and spine, forming the straight line from ear to heel that is desirable in all equitation.

with the horse, even if some days all you do is groom him. There is a chemistry that develops between the horse and rider, and it shows.

All of these things matter when you are in the ring.

. . . .

BILLY HARRIS

Billy Harris has been a judge more than forty years. At one time he had up to ten judge's cards, including for Quarter Horses, Appaloosas, Morgans, Pintos and Arabians. He now works exclusively with the Arabian breed. Harris is also a noted trainer and instructor.

In all classes, I want to see the basics done correctly, like the leads and smooth gait transitions. Beyond that, what I look for depends on the class.

In equitation classes, I look at the riders' feet and leg position first, then work up to the hip, shoulder and head.

A lot of riders have their weight in one stirrup more than the other, or roll their legs so they have more weight on the outside of the stirrup than on the inside.

The weight should be evenly in both stirrups. If the feet and legs are in good position, the rest of the body usually is, too. The rider should sit up tall, but not become rigid or tight (see illustrations, page 146 and below). The hand position should be balanced, and the fingers relaxed. Some riders try so hard to do everything perfectly that they tense up and take a death grip on the reins. That transmits to the horse's mouth.

I also like to see riders who have happy faces and are looking where they are going. I teach all my riders to look ahead. So many riders get into a bind because they don't look where they are going, and don't plan their moves or see what the other riders are doing. Riders must take into account the things happening around them. It's important to stay away from the crowds and any problems.

When the gaits are called, riders should take their time and pay attention to

This rider shows good Western Equitation form. If a line were dropped from the ear, it would pass through the center of the shoulder, center of the hip and back of the heel. The hand is balanced and the fingers relaxed.

position. Just because the announcer says to lope or jog, it doesn't mean they have to do it right away. It is better to wait for the right moment and concentrate on the transition.

I like to see riders stick close to the rail, regardless of the class. A good rider will be seen. Often parents coach their kids to go inside, but I want to see riders on the rail. That's where I look first to start picking horses.

The equitation horse should turn in a technically correct performance and move smoothly through the transitions. I judge a lot on transitions, and how the horse and rider handle them.

In the pattern I watch for smoothness of the execution, and how the rider coordinates the pattern's parts. If there are figure eights, I want to see all of the changes in the same spot. The rider should not go onto the rail when doing the eight. For rundowns, the horse should build up speed, rather than going slow then putting on a burst of speed. Each run should follow the tracks made by the last one.

It is essential for the rider to maintain form throughout and plan ahead. So many riders lose track of what they are doing and get kind of lost in the ring. When heading down to do a sliding stop, for example, the rider should already have planned when and where to stop the horse.

The rider should also be familiar with all of his or her equipment. This is one of my peeves. In Stock Seat Equitation, I see so many riatas that are on upside down, or coiled the wrong way. Some of the kids tell me, "My parents put it on." That doesn't matter. It is the rider's responsibility to understand all of the equipment and use it properly.

Riders should also continue to show the horse even in the lineup. When the judge moves down the line asking riders to back, they should prepare their horses before the judge reaches them, then back nice and straight.

The horse and rider should maintain form until they leave the arena. Some riders slump down and look like a sack of potatoes when they pick up their ribbons. That does not leave a good impression.

In English Pleasure (saddleseat type), the horse must have a lot of motion. He must be well balanced, bright, light in the bridle, and very athletic. He should also set up high in the bridle. One of the more common errors I see are horses with their heads dumped too far over.

In Western Pleasure, I want to see a horse in a balanced position, not with his head down and overflexed. For a long time many of the breeds were shown way too flexed. I fought that for years. The poll shouldn't drop below the withers. Rein contact should be light.

I like to see free, fluid, smooth motion. At the jog, I watch the back of the saddle. If it bangs around a lot on the back, I know the horse is rough even if the rider is handling it well. The horse should also be moving at a reasonable speed. Many go way too slow.

The horse should look happy in his work, like he is enjoying it. If I see a horse that is doing everything right but has his ears back, I'll still count down. I want to see that happy look. It is part of the pretty picture the horse must present. The horse should look like a Western Pleasure horse.

A mistake people often make is that they forget it is the horse—not them— that determines what he will be. They bring a horse to me or another trainer and say they want a stock horse, or a western horse or an English horse. I say let's work the horse and see what he wants to be. The talent and desire for the class have to be in the horse. You can't put it there.

We have a lot of good horses in the ring today, and good riders. I believe strongly in amateur riders. It is the amateurs who make the horse industry work.

The main thing I would tell amateurs who want to improve their riding is to ride as much as they can, and learn to relax and enjoy it. Have a good time at it. Some people are afraid they will mess up their horses if they ride a lot. But that's what the trainer is for. It's his or her job to keep the horse going. The more that people ride, the more they will learn.

That goes for showing as well. How they place isn't the most important thing. There is only one blue ribbon, and many horses. The most important thing is if they are happy with the ride. I tell my riders, "You have only one person to please, and that is you."

. . . .

KEN COPENHAVER

Ken Copenhaver has been judging since 1965, and has had his Quarter Horse card since 1977. His credits include being an open division judge at the American Quarter Horse Association World Championships. Copenhaver was the director of the equestrian program at Miami of Ohio University for thirteen years. He is also a riding instructor and trainer.

The best riders are the ones who come in knowing they are the best. It sounds somewhat arrogant, but it is not. They simply know that everyone else has to beat them, and it shows in the performance. If you can come in with that attitude, you can really make the judge watch you.

When you come through that gate, start showing immediately. In my case, the first time you go by me I'm going to begin placing you. If you make a bad pass the first time around, you are going to have to work much harder to get into the placings.

Pay attention to what you are doing in the ring and where you are. If you get covered up, the judge is not going to see you and is not going to look for you. It's your responsibility to stay as much in the open as you can. Create your spacing by going deep or shallow in the corners. I really don't like to see anyone circle. Most of the time when you circle, you end up in just as big a mess as you were in before.

The most important thing you can do to better your performances is to prepare. The quality of your ride depends on how much time you spend practicing, how you prepare the horse for the class, and your attitude and concentration during the class.

Showing the horse is an end product. You need to spend hours and hours of practice time with that horse before you go into the class. Part of the practice should be with the guidance of a professional who can tell you what you are doing right and what you are doing wrong. Accept the constructive criticism so you can find and fix your mistakes. Another good aid is to videotape your riding, then review the tape.

Lack of preparation is probably the single most common error I see as a judge.

If everything doesn't go just right, the unprepared horse and rider fall apart. For example, in a Horsemanship (Western Equitation) class, if the pattern is not the norm or they don't practice a lot of patterns, it shows up pretty fast. The riders get flustered, and maybe they'll start looking down or their heels will come up. Good riding should be a habit. If you practice good form, it will always be with you without your having to think about it. When you encounter problems or are asked for something out of the ordinary, your form will stay intact.

Another thing that shows up is uncertainty. I can see the uncertainty in the riders' faces. They look nervous. Their bodies are very stiff, and there's no give in the hands. Everything about them says how unsure they are. They don't glance over at the judge. Often they'll look down, and that causes their head to drop and their shoulders to round.

The cure for uncertainty is experience and practice. Try to come in with confidence, and prepared for what the class will bring. Know your horse and his abilities. If you show your horse to his best ability, you'll do just fine.

In Hunt Seat Equitation, I want to see the riders looking where they are going and sitting erect with no bow in their backs. In equitation, everything is straight lines—a straight line from your ear to your shoulder to your hip and to your heel, and a straight line from your elbow to the horse's mouth (see illustration, page 151). The hands must be about 30 degrees off the perpendicular, not horizontal or with the wrists bent. The rein contact should be light, with no slack. Slack in the rein in Hunt Seat is a definite no-no.

The leg should be steady and on the horse. I often ask riders to drop their stirrups, especially in the pattern. That really brings to the top the good riders who are in shape. The first circle of the figure eight, most do pretty good, but the second one you can see a lot of them fade. You have to be in good physical shape to ride these horses. That means staying in shape, and not staying out half the night partying if you are going to show the next day. Being prepared means being physically and mentally ready to go when that gate opens.

In Horsemanship, I look for very similar things as with Hunt Seat Equitation. I want the same steady leg, with the heel down. I want the same line from the ear to the heel, the same erectness in the body. I also want to see patterns that are crisp and well planned.

Good Hunt Seat Equitation form is straight lines—a line from ear to shoulder to hip to heel, and a line from the rider's elbow to the horse's mouth.

A rider can come in on a $500 horse and have just as much a chance as the rider on a $20,000 horse if he or she has everything else put together. It is judged 100 percent on the rider, and if the rider does a good job he or she is going to place well.

A smile is nice if it is natural, but don't paste on a big toothy grin. Some people work so hard on smiling that everything else falls apart. Many riders concentrating on their riding do not smile, and that is fine.

Common flaws I see in Horsemanship are too much slack in the reins, the rider not having a straight line from elbow to the horse's mouth and the hands being flat (turned over so that the thumb faces sideways instead of up). I also see riders who fall apart in the patterns. They tend to put their feet too far forward. Some also drop their eyes, which causes them to round their whole body forward.

After the class, I'm more than happy to talk to riders about how they did, and tell them what I did and did not like. When I do Horsemanship, Equitation and Showmanship, I write down something on every person in the ring.

In all classes, clothing and tack are important. They don't have to be fancy, but they do have to fit well, be appropriate for the class and be clean. To know if you have appropriate clothing and tack, look at your competitors. Follow that style. Also, if you've got silver, make sure it is spotless. I hate seeing someone come in with a $6,000 to $7,000 saddle with tarnished silver. That tells me he or she didn't put enough time in preparation. It leaves a bad impression.

In Western Pleasure, I want to see the horse come in alert, and look like he is enjoying what he is doing. His head set should be vertical, and his neck horizontal or a little above. If I see the horse's neck below the horizontal, and his face inside the vertical, I'm going to count him down as much as I possibly can.

I want to see the horse walk like he is going somewhere, not creep along. I use the walk as a gait to be judged, not a rest period. At the jog, I want to see the horse move naturally, and with a flat knee (not much flex). He should use his hindquarters well and stay under himself. The same is true of the canter. I don't want to see him four-beating.

If you are riding a big horse, he is going to cover more ground than a small horse. That's fine. Judges understand that the larger horse has a longer stride that covers the ground faster. More important than speed is if the horse is moving within his frame—in other words, if he is moving at a speed appropriate for his size. It is fine to pass other riders if your horse is larger or longer-strided. You shouldn't try to make a 16-hand horse move like a 14.2 horse or he'll be really choppy looking. The training methods it may take to get him to move that way may also make him afraid of the rider. I don't want to see a horse intimidated by his rider.

The horse should look content, and be clean, healthy and in good physical condition, with adequate weight for his size.

In hunter classes, I want to see the horse trot with a very flat knee, with no animation. He should cover the ground like he is going somewhere, but not trot fast. It used to be that the faster the horse trotted, the better, but that isn't true anymore. He should move at a nice speed for his size and length of stride.

He should appear content with himself, and not carry his neck below the horizontal or his face inside the vertical. I like to see the horse be bright, and listening to the rider. It's fine if he puts an ear back to listen, but I don't want to see the ears pinned.

. . . .

DAVID MCKAY

David McKay has been an American Horse Show Association licensed judge since 1974, and judges Arabians on a national level, Saddlebreds, Morgans, open western divisions and some hunter jumpers.

A common error I see is riders trying to make last-minute changes at the horse show. They worry about the other riders in the ring and sometimes try to imitate them. This trait exemplifies itself in many ways. One is excess speed. A rider will see a horse with a long stride perform with what apparently is a faster trot, and subsequently will try to copy that motion. Many times that leads to an untrue gait.

The major suggestion I can give to amateurs is to trust their own horse and their ability to ride. If they are consistent and perform to their best ability, they will usually place better in the class. Don't make sudden last-minute changes. If changes are necessary, plenty of time should be given for the transition. Reviewing videotapes of rides with knowledgeable horse people will help correct many hidden faults not felt or previously seen by the rider. Suitability of horse and rider is also paramount when showing any breed of horse.

The most important thing a rider can do to improve his or her riding is to practice often with good, knowledgeable people, and practice with a purpose in mind.

Discipline and demonstrating smoothness in changing gaits are two qualities that the good riders share. These riders stand out in a crowd. They exhibit the ability to keep the horse out of trouble, and show organization in their ring deportment. Performing the gaits as specified in the rule book is extremely important.

The best equitation riders are those who demonstrate horsemanship. They are in control of the horse and their surroundings at all times. They know correct positioning in the show ring, and discipline of the horse. They are not just passengers with a pretty smile, but are capable of handling any situation with the utmost ease and dexterity.

All good western horses, regardless of breed, demonstrate good working attitudes. The attitude is observed by relaxed motion in the gaits, suppleness in working of the hindquarters and ease of handling in reining. The horse is relaxed, showing no signs of discomfort, and has a willingness to perform.

The good huntseat horses demonstrate a highly efficient working attitude with a willingness to move forward regardless of the terrain. They must be alert and show a driving motion to cover distance with little effort. These horses should appear to be trusted and safe. This class is for the show ring but derives its origin from the woods and mountains, and thus hunters should show soundness and a true way of going.

WHAT YOU CAN DO RIGHT AWAY TO IMPROVE

- Read your rule book so you understand the rules and the standards of performance you are being judged by.
- Become familiar with all of your equipment.
- Seek the advice and guidance of knowledgeable people.

WHAT YOU CAN DO IN THE FUTURE

- Talk to the judges at shows after your classes are over.
- Review videotapes of your rides with knowledgeable horse people.
- Practice with an eye toward perfecting your form and that of the horse in every gait, and through the transitions.
- Treat each class like it is the most important of your life. Do the best grooming and preparation possible every time. Strive to give the best performance you can and show the horse from the minute you enter the ring until after you have left the arena.

Resource Guide

Many of the resources you need to improve your knowledge and skills with horses are already available to you. You just have to know where to look.

Opportunities abound in the form of equine organizations, social events, clinics, farms, shows and people. You can learn a great deal by being an active participant in the horse community.

Events

Events such as open houses, sales and other social activities at horse farms and horse shows offer you a great opportunity to see horses and meet other horse people. When you go, make it a point to meet the host and spend at least part of the time talking with people you previously did not know. If you cling to the groups you know, you won't meet anyone new.

The connections you make can be mutually beneficial. Together you become a kind of informal network. Through it, you can find or market horses, meet trainers and riding instructors and exchange information. These are the people you'll turn to at the shows when you break a piece of tack and need to borrow another, or who you will loan grooming supplies after they run out. There really is a horse community. It is tied together by its equine interests rather than geographical boundaries. You are a part of this community. Make an effort to meet the other residents. Among these people you will find friends, teachers and perhaps even a mentor to help guide your horse efforts.

Keep abreast of the horse shows coming to your region and attend the ones you can. You can learn a great deal even as a spectator, especially at high-level shows.

Good learning opportunities also include clinics. They offer intensive instruction and can give you new insights. Some are taught by the country's top instructors or trainers. Make it a point to attend those that come to your area. If for some reason you cannot ride in them, go as a spectator.

Media

Equine books, magazines and instructional videos are excellent sources of information on a variety of topics.

Visit your local library and bookstores for books relating to classes of interest and general horse care. Start building a personal library of instructional books.

Subscribe to at least one horse magazine. If you are showing in breed shows, it is a good idea to subscribe to a magazine specifically for your breed, as well as a general equine magazine. It will allow you to see what the top horses look like and help you keep track of trends in the industry, performance, grooming, etc.

Contact your horse organization to see if they have a video lending library. A list of national organizations is at the end of this chapter. Some large breeding farms have videos to lend as well. Many of these organizations and farm videos are excellent. It's like having a front-row seat at a clinic without ever leaving your living room.

Adult and Family Groups

Considering all the horse lovers there are in the world, it's no wonder that nearly every community has at least one horse-oriented organization. These groups can offer you a range of educational, social and riding opportunities.

To find the right group, ask around among horse people to see what is available. You can also call the national headquarters for your breed of choice and ask about chapters in your area. A listing of many of the breed associations is at the end of this chapter. Your state's horse council may also have a listing of some groups in your area.

Organizations available will depend on your age as well as location. Some groups tend to focus more on social events and fun rides but not on showing. Others are oriented more toward showing and educational activities. You may want to attend a few meetings of various organizations, then pick the one that suits you best.

Through the group you can accomplish many things. You have the ability to move it in the direction you would like it to go. The organization can be a vehicle for you to enrich your horse experience and offer that enrichment to others in the organization as well.

Most people in groups would like them to be more active, but don't know what to do. That's an opportunity for you to take the lead and do some of the things you would like. There are some activities that are easier or less expensive to accomplish as part of a group. The barrier that keeps groups from doing interesting things is not lack of desire. It usually is just that no one wants to take the initiative and do the work that goes with it.

For example, say you are in an equine group that is largely social. That is good in itself, because it brings you in contact with other horse people. If you can join a group that has members showing on the level you wish to be, it is better yet. Any opportunity to meet and talk with people who have already found success will be helpful to you.

But your social club doesn't have to just be social. The organization can give you the backing to do all kinds of things.

Perhaps there are some horse farms you have always wanted to see. In your next meeting, ask if anyone would be interested in a field trip there, then offer to arrange it. Many farms are receptive to giving group tours and showing off some of their more well-known horses. And field trips don't have to be just limited to farms. You can visit veterinary schools, too, or other places.

Or you might propose arranging a speaker for one meeting. You, of course, would suggest someone that you have always wanted to meet. Arranging this gives you a forum in which you can do this and also helps further the education of your group. If the group is receptive, give the person a call. Also offer to escort the guest to the meeting. That will give you more time to get acquainted.

You might also rent an instructional video for the group. Group rates are usually fairly inexpensive and occasionally free.

If you are feeling extremely ambitious, talk to your group about bringing in a respected horse professional to put on a clinic. You would gather facts such as the number of people interested in attending the clinic, where it could be held, the price of the facility, if the professional is available and his or her clinic price.

If it looked like the clinic could be successful and not a financial drain, chances are the organization would approve it. You could then attend the clinic with the professional of your choice. Don't assume such a person would never come to your city. You have the ability to make it happen. If you wanted to spend even more time with that person, you could offer to ferry him or her around during the stay. The two of you could get to know each other and talk shop.

You could also arrange mini-clinics that are more like hour-long group lessons with local riding instructors on a regular basis. This is a less imposing task than putting on a clinic but will help your riding skill and that of other members. Group lessons would also be less costly for you than individual lessons, so mixing in a few with individual lessons can be good for the budget. Your horse would also get more practice in a group setting that simulates the show ring. But keep the group sessions small. Too many horses, and no one will get much individualized attention. Ask the instructor what the best number of horses and riders would be for him or her to teach.

The key to making all of these things happen is simple—offer to do them. You won't get anywhere by suggesting it then hoping someone else will do it for you. By offering to do the bulk of the work yourself, you usually can get the support of the group fairly quickly.

Youth Groups

Most youth groups are heavily structured for education and improvement of riding skills. The youth groups offer a good range of opportunities and information for a person who is starting out in the horse world and is eighteen or under. They cover the basics of horse care, safety and riding, and do a lot of fun things you can enjoy with other horse people.

Among the most widespread equine youth groups are 4-H and Pony Club.

The 4-H program covers a myriad of topics, with horses being one. It is a good, basic program for youths through age eighteen. There are chapters in nearly every town in the United States. To locate your local chapter, look in the phone book under county offices for the Extension Service. It manages the National 4-H programs. You can also write at the address listed on page 161, or call for information.

Pony Club is an international organization for youth with ponies or horses of any breed. It is another good basic program and emphasizes English riding skills required for dressage and jumping. In the United States, the groups are run through United States Pony Clubs, Inc. To get information about your local chapter, ask around among horse people or write to the address listed on page 162.

Also available to people under eighteen are youth associations that are part of large breed organizations. These include the American Junior Quarter Horse Association, which has as 12,000 members internationally.

You can get a lot from these organizations if you take advantage of what is offered. Read the information given to you, participate in the lessons and clinics, go on the field trips, serve as an officer, go to the higher-level shows offered by the group. If you just cruise through it all, you won't learn much.

Making the Extra Effort

Being active in a club is important, but it is also important to continue working on your own behalf as well. Becoming a skilled and knowledgeable rider takes extra effort. Riders who work on their equine skills only as part of a group rarely advance very far. Organizations can enhance your skills, but should not replace your initiative.

This is particularly true with organizations that include riding instruction and practice. Most of these lessons take place in groups. This can give you a feel of what it will be like in the show ring faced with crowding and horses going different speeds. The problem is that if the practice group is large you will not receive a great deal of instruction. There are too many people for the instructor to watch and advise. The instructor also will naturally gravitate to giving the most help to the people with the most obvious problems. If you are doing okay, you may not hear much from him or her.

But you want to be more than okay. It takes more than okay to excel in a class. You need extra help to boost you into the ranks of the successful.

Part of that help could come from your group instructor. If you believe the instructor is fairly knowledgeable, after the group sessions ask if the instructor would be willing to stay a little longer and work with you individually. Most instructors in groups are volunteers and are willing to do this. Have in mind specifically the area you want to work on when you make the request. Specific requests, such as "Could you help me with transitions? I'm having trouble bringing my horse down from a trot to a walk without him poking out his nose," lead to more beneficial sessions than general requests for help.

Be aware, however, that the quality of the instruction you receive in the group is only as good the person giving it. If the instructor is knowledgeable, he or she can help you a lot in becoming a better rider. If the instructor is limited, the things you learn will be limited, too. Don't assume that just because the person is teaching that he or she knows a great deal. That may not be the case. There are many instructors who are not qualified to teach anything more than basic riding.

In addition to your work within the group, also work on your own and with other horse professionals. The extra effort will show itself in greater success in the ring.

Organizations

The following are some of the horse associations that may be of use to you. For information on joining or on educational services provided, write or call:

American Association of Owners and Breeders of Peruvian Paso Horses: P.O. Box 30723, Oakland, CA 94604. Phone: 415-636-1049.

American Horse Council: 1700 K Street Northwest, Suite 300, Washington, DC 20006-3805. Phone: 202 296-4031. A national trade organization for the horse industry in the United States, the council can provide a variety of information about the industry and various breed associations.

American Horse Shows Association: 220 East 42nd Street, New York, NY 10017-5876. Phone: 212-972-2472. The national governing body of equestrian sport in the United States, AHSA writes the rules and regulations of the show ring.

American Morgan Horse Association: P.O. Box 960, Shelburne, VT 05482-0960. Phone: 802-985-4944.

American Paint Horse Association: P.O. Box 961023, Fort Worth, TX 76161-0023. Phone: 817-439-3400.

American Quarter Horse Association: 2701 I-40 East, Amarillo, TX 79168. Phone: 806-376-4811.

American Saddlebred Horse Association: 4093 Iron Works Pike, Lexington, KY 40511. Phone: 606-259-2742.

Appaloosa Horse Club, Inc.: P.O. Box 8403, Moscow, ID, 83843-0903. Phone: 208-882-5578.

Canadian Equestrian Federation: 1600 James Naismith Drive, Gloucester, Ontario K1B 5N4, Canada. Phone: 613-748-5632. The national governing body of equestrian sport in Canada, CEF writes the rules and regulations of the show ring.

Canadian Horse Council: P.O. Box 156, 555 Rexdale Boulevard, Rexdale, Ontario M9W 5L2, Canada. Phone: 416-675-6110. A trade organization for the horse industry in Canada, the council can provide a variety of information on the industry and on horse associations in Canada.

International Arabian Horse Association: P.O. Box 33696, Denver, CO 80233-0696. Phone: 303-450-4774.

National 4-H Council: 7100 Connecticut Avenue, Chevy Chase, MD 20815. Phone: 301-961-2945.

National Show Horse Registry: 11700 Commonwealth Drive, No. 200, Louisville, KY 40299. Phone: 502-266-5100. The registry and organization for the National Show Horse breed.

North American Warmblood Association: 2400 Faussett Road, Howell, MI 48843. Phone: 517-546-5280.

Paso Fino Horse Association: 100 West Main Street, P.O. Box 600, Bowling Green, FL 33834-0600. Phone:. 813-375-4331.

Pony of the Americas Club (POAs): 5240 Elmwood Avenue, Indianapolis, IN 46203-5990. Phone: 317-788-0107.

Tennessee Walking Horse Breeders' and Exhibitors' Association: P.O. Box 286, Lewisburg, TN 37091-0286. Phone: 615-359-1574.

United States Pony Clubs, Inc.: 4071 Ironworks Pike, National Horse Center, Kentucky Horse Park, Lexington, KY 40511. Phone: 606-254-7669.

Welsh Pony and Cob Society of America: P.O. Box 2977, Winchester, VA 22601-2977. Phone: 703-667-6195.

WHAT YOU CAN DO RIGHT AWAY TO IMPROVE

- Write or call the association for your breed of choice and ask about educational materials it can provide, including videos.
- Look into various horse organizations to see which you may want to join.
- Subscribe to a magazine appropriate for your level of riding and interests.
- Check out what horse books your local library and bookstores have.

WHAT YOU CAN DO IN THE FUTURE

- Join a horse organization if you are not already in one.
- Participate in planning at least one educational club event in the next year, such as going on a field trip, putting on a clinic or ordering a video.
- Become a regular reader of horse books and magazines. They offer an inexpensive and easy way to learn a great deal about riding and horses.
- Attend available clinics, horse-related social events and shows.

Keeping Records

The final aspect in showing a horse well is keeping good records.

When you return home from the horse show, jot down how you did in each class while your memory is still fresh. Accurate show records provide good information to refer back to and can also be helpful when marketing a horse.

Keep records, too, on the judges you show under. By noting their tastes, you can potentially improve your placings by adapting to their preferences somewhat. When you are deciding what shows to attend, you can also look up the judge in your records to see how he or she treated you last time. You can avoid judges who placed you poorly, and instead patronize shows with judges who favor your horse.

Judge Records

Every judge has horses he or she likes or dislikes. When a judge dislikes your horse, it doesn't mean that he or she is a bad judge or that you have a bad horse. It's just the opinion of one man or woman. The horse did not fall within the judge's preferences. It happens occasionally to everyone. A month before one of my horses won a national championship, I took him to a small breed show and could scarcely win a ribbon. The judge was a learned, well-respected man. He just happened to dislike that particular horse's way of going.

When you come across a judge who does not like your horse, make note of it in your records and avoid showing under him or her with that horse in the future. Note the judges who like your horse as well. Showing takes a lot of time and effort. There are also lots of shows to choose from. You might as well show at those with judges who favor your horse, rather than with those who don't.

Take care when you are making these assessments of the judge that you take into account how well the horse performed in the classes. If the horse was naughty and you didn't place, it's not fair to say the judge didn't like him. The horse didn't give the judge the chance to like him. Make your assessments over time. Also remember that just because the judge dislikes or likes one of your horses, it doesn't mean he will have the same opinion about the next one. As you show, the judge's preferences will become increasingly clear and you will develop a better understanding of what he or she wants in a horse and in a performance.

For your judge records, you can copy the form in this chapter or make your own (see illustration, page 165). The record should contain the following:
- Judge's name and where he or she is from.
- The type of placings you usually receive.
- The shows where you had him or her. This will be a list that you can add to as you show.
- The judge's preferences at every gait. This would be such things as if he or she likes the western jog extremely slow or slightly faster, if horses are penalized for a walk too slow, if he or she likes heads deeply tucked or slightly out.

JUDGE RECORD

Judge _____   Address _____

_____

Shows: _____

_____

_____

_____

Average placings (excellent) (good) (average) (poor) (none)

Judge's preferences:

Walk _____

_____

Jog/Trot _____

_____

Canter/Lope _____

_____

Rider's qualities _____

_____

Pattern _____

_____

Other _____

_____

_____

Comments:

Use a record like this to track judges and their preferences.

- For equitation classes, also note the qualities of riders the judge favored, if a pattern was requested and what it was.
- Room for any other comments you may have.
  Keep your records in a loose-leaf binder, a notebook or on computer so you can add to it.

Show Records

Show records contain the statistics of the show—what classes you entered and how you did. They don't take a lot of time to do, and can be helpful to you. They can also be fun to look through and reminisce over.

For your records, you can copy the form in this book, or make your own (see illustration, page 167). The form should include:

- The horse's name and, if you wish, other statistical information such as the sire, dam, breed, sex, owner and rider.
- The show, and when and where it was held.
- The judge's name.
- The classes and how you placed. Include even those in which you received nothing. Knowing how often you didn't place can help you see how far you've progressed once you begin placing frequently.
- The number of horses in the class. Whether you got first, second or third in a class isn't the whole story. It is a greater accomplishment to receive fifth in a class of forty than to win a class of three.
- Winnings. Put down the money and other awards you win, such as trophies, tack and silver platters. This can be a lot of fun to track and will also help you remember where you got each award. In classes, I've received everything from dessert forks to bronze sculptures and paintings.
- Comments. This section serves as a kind of diary. Put in it anything that impressed you about the horse's performances, the show, grounds, what the weather was, how you felt, and so on.

SHOW RECORD

Horse _____

Sex ____ Breed _____ Sire _____ Dam _____

Owner _____ Rider _____

Show _____ Date _____

Location _____ Judge _____

Classes   Placing   No. of Horses

_____

_____

_____

_____

_____

_____

_____

_____

_____

_____

_____

Winnings _____

_____

Comments _____

_____

_____

_____

Use a form like this to record your show placings.

WHAT YOU CAN DO RIGHT AWAY TO IMPROVE

- Copy the forms in this chapter and begin your records today. Your show record will become a testimony to your dedication as a rider. It will serve as a tangible reminder of the progress you have made. As it grows, you will be able to see how far you have come.

WHAT YOU CAN DO IN THE FUTURE

- Develop a belief in yourself, the horse and your ability to succeed.
- Through the good times and the bad, hold on to your dedication to improving your riding skills and equine education. It will lead you to the winner's circle.

  Becoming a winning rider takes time and hard work. But everything you have done—the careful selection of the horse, practices, lessons, grooming and care—carries you closer to realizing your dreams of show ring success.

Index

Numbers in *italics* indicate illustrations.